SHELLFISH

Other books in
The Particular Palate Cookbook™ Series

GARLIC
by Sue Kreitzman

RIBS
by Susan Friedland

TAILGATE PARTIES
by Susan Wyler

COOKIES
by Diane Rozas and Rosalee Harris

DELI
by Sue Kreitzman

CHICKEN BREASTS
by Diane Rozas

CHOCOLATE CANDY
by Anita Prichard

COMFORT FOOD
by Sue Kreitzman

FISH STEAKS AND FILLETS
by Michele Scicolone

POTATOES
by Sue Kreitzman

SAUCES AND DRESSINGS
by Diane Rozas

SHELLFISH

85 recipes for
lobsters, shrimp, scallops,
crabs, clams, mussels,
oysters, and squid

by Michele Scicolone

A Particular Palate Cookbook™
Harmony Books/New York

Copyright © 1989 by Michele Scicolone

Published by Harmony Books, a division of Crown Publishers, Inc., 201 East 50th Street, New York, New York 10022

HARMONY, PARTICULAR PALATE, and colophon are trademarks of Crown Publishers, Inc.

Manufactured in the United States of America

Illustrations by Jennifer Harper

Library of Congress Cataloging-in-Publication Data

Scicolone, Michele.
    Shellfish: 85 recipes for lobsters, shrimp, scallops, crabs, clams, mussels, oysters, and squid / by Michele Scicolone.
        p.   cm.
    "A particular palate cookbook."
    Includes index.
    1. Cookery (Shellfish) I. Title.
    TX753.S36   1989   89-11021
    641.6′94—dc20   CIP

ISBN 0-517-57337-7

10 9 8 7 6 5 4 3 2 1
First Edition

Contents

Introduction

Shellfish on the menu turns an ordinary meal into a special occasion. A casual backyard barbecue, an intimate dinner for two, or an informal dinner with family and friends becomes a feast when shellfish is served.

Why is shellfish so appealing? First of all, it looks so good—the varied shapes and colors are endlessly fascinating. Then, too, eating it is an adventure. Crabs and lobsters, for instance, offer a challenge to the eater, who, equipped with oyster fork, nutpick, nutcracker, and mallet, must first get through their unyielding armor to reach the choice, juicy meat. And there is romance—a shellfish dinner conjures up thoughts of sun-drenched days and balmy nights at the shore, even if it is served in the middle of winter. But, most of all, the incomparable taste and texture of sweet, tender lobsters, scallops, shrimp, and crabs, briny mussels, oysters, and clams, and exotic squid make a shellfish dinner unforgettable.

Shellfish is not difficult to prepare. Because its natural flavors are so delicate and distinctive, the best way to serve most varieties is as simply as possible. In this book you will find all you need to know about selecting fresh shellfish, preparing it for cooking, cooking techniques, and how to serve it. Tender shellfish does not need long cooking, and most recipes in this book require less than 30 minutes of cooking time.

Some of the recipes I've included are old favorites, but there are also lots of new ideas, too. Fresh, unprocessed ingredients that are readily available are used whenever possible. Since most people seem to be watching what they eat these days, many of the recipes are low in calories, though there are a sufficient number of treats for when you feel like splurging.

Speaking of splurging, there is no denying that many shellfish are expensive. But you will find many recipes and hints that stretch a small amount of shellfish a long way without sacrificing flavor. There is also an abundance of recipes for inexpensive yet delicious shellfish like mussels and squid. And keep in mind that eating shellfish at home is more economical than ordering it in a restaurant.

The next time you are looking for something different to make for yourself, family, or friends, make shellfish and make something special.

A FEW WORDS ABOUT INGREDIENTS

Crab Boil: A mixture of spices good for seasoning a variety of shellfish, it can be purchased in supermarkets or fish markets. If unavailable, use a combination of ground red pepper, paprika, minced garlic, salt, and pepper.

Lemon Juice: Always use freshly squeezed lemon juice. Bottled lemon juice, frozen or otherwise, has an unpleasant chemical taste that does not complement any food, especially delicate shellfish. I keep fresh lemons on hand at all times. Place them in the vegetable crisper of the refrigerator and they will keep well for several weeks. Don't leave them in a plastic bag, or they may become moldy. You can extract more juice from a room-temperature lemon than a cold one, so take them out of the refrigerator before using. If you are going to grate the lemon peel, do it before squeezing the juice. An average lemon yields about 3 tablespoons of juice. Fresh limes often can be substituted for lemons.

Tomatoes: Tomatoes complement the flavor of shellfish and are used in many of the recipes in this book. The best type for cooking are the meaty plum-shaped tomatoes sometimes called Roma tomatoes. These have a full tomato flavor and a minimum of seeds and juice, so they cook down to a delicious sauce. So far as peeling is concerned, it is not necessary for salads and sautéed dishes, though it is a good idea for delicate sauces. To peel tomatoes, drop them into a pot of boiling water for 30 seconds, keeping them submerged with a spoon. Remove the tomatoes and let them cool slightly. Slit the skin and remove it with a sharp paring knife. Cut the tomato in half and remove the core. Squeeze it gently to extract the seeds and juice.

WHICH WINE?

Shellfish and white wines are natural companions. The acid in white wine complements shellfish in the same way as a squeeze of fresh lemon juice. It perks up the flavor and at the same time cleanses the palate so that you are ready to eat more.

Red wine, on the other hand, rarely works with shellfish. The tannin in red wine often brings out an unpleasant metallic flavor. The only exceptions that I have found are when shellfish is cooked in a tomato-based sauce, but even then a crisp, dry white wine would be my first choice.

Clams, mussels, and oysters have a briny taste that works well with Muscadet or Chablis and Pinot Grigio. Slightly sweet crabs, scallops, squid, shrimp, and lobsters are good with Pouilly-Fumé, Saint Veran, or California Sauvignon Blanc.

The manner in which the shellfish is prepared has a big influence on the choice of wine. While cold lobster salad may go well with a Sauvignon Blanc, hot lobster with butter would be better with a fuller-flavored wine like California Chardonnay. For special occasions, you can't go wrong with lobster and Champagne!

When fresh tomatoes are not in season, I use canned tomatoes imported from Italy. The better brands are vine-ripened and when cooked have a flavor and texture much like the fresh, and sometimes better. Read the can labels carefully to determine their origin. Many cans state that the contents are "Italian style," which means that they were actually grown elsewhere. Often these tomatoes are watery and hard and may require longer cooking.

A FEW WORDS ABOUT EQUIPMENT

Oyster Knife: There are all kinds of gadgets on the market that may be used to open oysters. Some people like to use a "church-key" type of can opener, and others prefer a long-bladed knife. But to me the best, and the safest for beginners, is a short-bladed knife with a sturdy plastic or wooden handle. The blade is fairly wide and comes to a sharp, pointed tip, something like a lopsided arrowhead. Many oyster knives have a narrow cuff between the blade and the handle, which helps to protect your fingers from the sharp edges of the oyster shell.

Clam Knife: Clam knives are quite different from oyster knives. They have a longer blade to accommodate the width of a large clam, and a rounded tip. One side of their broad blade is sharp, while the other is blunt. A good clam knife should have a full tang, meaning that its blade extends through the length of the handle, making it strong enough to pry open a reluctant clam without breaking.

SHELLFISH SAFETY

From time to time we hear or read reports of outbreaks of illnesses, mainly gastrointestinal, that can be traced to eating shellfish. Usually the culprit is raw shellfish that was harvested in polluted waters or areas contaminated by "red tides," a naturally occurring poisonous algae.

It is important to remember that all unpasteurized or raw foods carry a greater degree of risk of contamination. For this reason, milk and other dairy products are pasteurized before they are sold, and pork and chicken should be thoroughly cooked before consumption.

To prevent illness, buy shellfish only from a reputable market. "Farmed" shellfish is probably safer to eat than "wild" or natural shellfish, since the farmed products are inspected regularly, which may not be the case with wild shellfish. Check that local shellfish come from uncontaminated waters by contacting your regional department of health. Learn to recognize fresh shellfish by reading the introduction to each chapter in this book. At home, store shellfish properly and keep it well chilled. Thaw frozen shellfish in the refrigerator or under cold running water. Remember that cooking kills many harmful bacteria, though it may not kill all. If you have any doubts about the quality of any shellfish, don't eat it. Persons with preexisting health problems are more likely than healthy people to become ill from tainted shellfish and probably would do well to avoid it and similar raw foods altogether.

Crackers, Mallets, and Picks: The hard shells and tiny crevices of lobsters and crabs require some special tools to open them. Inexpensive nutcrackers and nutpicks, available at any good housewares store, are very effective for digging out the meat of lobsters and crabs. Be sure that they are made of metal strong enough not to bend. Metal crackers are also easy to clean. A small wooden or metal mallet is useful for cracking tough crab and lobster legs, but a meat-tenderizing mallet will do the job.

Tongs: A pair of long-handled metal tongs is very useful for cooking shellfish. It makes removing lobsters or crabs from steaming water easy and is also helpful for deep frying.

Deep Fryer and Frying Thermometer: If you do a lot of deep frying, an electric fryer is a good investment. Most models have markings that indicate the correct oil level, and all regulate the temperature so that food is cooked crisp and greaseless. Choose one with a frying basket that makes it easy to place food in the oil without splashing. Also good are covered fryers. Not only are they safer to operate, the cover helps to control the odor of the fried foods.

If you don't have an electric fryer, do invest in a good deep-frying thermometer. Many of these thermometers can do double duty for candy making and take the guesswork out of maintaining the perfect temperature, critical for fried foods.

A FEW WORDS ABOUT THE RECIPES

Serving Sizes: Although I have given a number of servings for each recipe, remember that these figures are averages. If there are a number of other dishes on the menu, or appetites are small, obviously the recipes will serve more. If appetites are hearty and you will want to offer seconds, figure on fewer servings per recipe.

KEEPING THEM STRAIGHT

When serving oysters, mussels, and clams on the half shell, it is important to keep the shells level so that they don't tip and lose the precious juices that make them moist and flavorful. To serve them cold, place a bed of crushed ice on the serving plates and set the shells into it. This will keep the shellfish well chilled, too.

For baked oysters, mussels, and clams, there are several alternatives. One possibility is rock salt, which should be spread about ½ inch thick in a shallow roasting pan or jelly roll pan. Preheat the salt-filled pan in the oven about 15 minutes before setting the shellfish on top. This will not only prevent tipping but also keep them warm for serving. Be very careful not to get any of the salt into the shells.

Another possibility is to crumple slightly some aluminum foil and lay it in the bottom of the pan. It, too, will hold the shellfish upright in the pan. Easiest of all is a wire rack, such as a cake-cooling rack. Balance the shells between the wires and they will stay level.

Substitutions: Don't hesitate to make substitutions in these recipes. For example, if you happen to be out of a particular herb, try another in its place. Consider the other ingredients and decide if the flavors would work together. Chances are they will, and the recipe will have your personal touch.

Many of these recipes call for dry white wine, but other liquids can be substituted, such as dry white vermouth (in slightly smaller quantities), beer, clam juice, fish stock, chicken or vegetable broth, or even water.

Often, too, you can substitute one shellfish for another. Many of the oyster, mussel, and clam recipes are interchangeable, as are those for lobster and crab.

AQUACULTURE

The word *aquaculture* is another term for farm-raising fish and shellfish. The idea of a farm for mussels, oysters, shrimp, and other shellfish may seem strange, but it is a booming industry around the world—for a good reason. Increasing demands for fresh seafood have placed a strain on the naturally available supply. Some species have become scarce, while others are on the verge of extinction from overfishing.

Grown in a controlled environment, farmed shellfish is protected from hazards such as chemical spills, bad weather, and pollution. As a result, it is of consistently high quality and available all year round. On the whole, it is cleaner and fresher-tasting than wild shellfish. Farm-raised mussels, for example, are practically free of sand and grit. The shells are thinner and are less likely to be covered with barnacles, so you actually get more mussels per pound.

Aquaculture has also made available varieties of shellfish that were rarely seen before. French Belon oysters, for example, are delicious, but shipping costs across the Atlantic made prices prohibitive. Now Belons are being cultivated in North America, and with great success.

Although farm-raised shellfish may be slightly more expensive than the wild, it is well worth the price difference for its cleanliness, variety, and availability.

SHELLFISH NUTRITION

Shellfish is naturally low in calories yet high in protein. It is also a rich source of many vitamins and important minerals such as iron and calcium.

Recent studies have shown that shellfish is not as high in cholesterol as was once thought. There are two kinds of shellfish: mollusks and crustaceans. Bivalve mollusks—those that have two shells, such as clams, oysters, scallops, and mussels—are actually low in cholesterol. Crustaceans, which include lobsters, crabs, and shrimp, are generally higher in cholesterol, although a 3½-ounce serving contains far less than the 275 mg of cholesterol found in one egg yolk. Even squid (which is in the mollusk family), with its "high" cholesterol content, has less cholesterol than one egg yolk.

The following figures are for the most common varieties of each shellfish and are based upon 3½ ounces (100 grams) shelled before cooking. Exact nutrient values will vary slightly depending on the specific variety, where it grows, its age, the season, and other factors. Note that the sodium levels of some processed shellfish such as crab may be higher than indicated, because salt is often added in the processing technique.

PER 3½ OUNCES Raw Edible Portion	CALORIES	PROTEIN Milligrams	SODIUM Milligrams	CHOLESTEROL Milligrams
Clams	74	12.77	56	34
Crabs	87	18.06	293	78
Lobsters	90	18.80	177	95
Mussels	86	11.90	286	28
Oysters	69	7.06	112	55
Scallops	88	16.78	161	33
Shrimp	106	20.31	148	152
Squid	92	15.58	44	233

Clams

"But when that smoking chowder came in, the mystery was delightfully explained. Oh! sweet friends, hearken to me. It was made of small juicy clams, scarcely bigger than hazelnuts, mixed with pounded ship's biscuits and salted pork cut up into little flakes, the whole enriched with butter, and plentifully seasoned with pepper and salt...."

Herman Melville,
Moby Dick

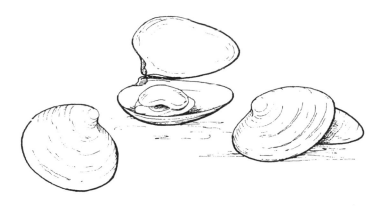

Most clams can be divided into two categories: hard shell and soft shell. Hard shell clams are named according to their size. The smallest are called littlenecks and are very tender. Littlenecks are best served raw on the half shell, but they may also be baked or steamed. Cherrystones are medium-size clams. Most often cherrystones are served stuffed and baked, but they can also be eaten steamed or raw on the half shell. Chowder clams, sometimes called quahogs (pronounced co-hogs), are the largest and toughest of the hard shell clams. Chowder clams are usually chopped or cut into strips for use in chowders or as fried clams.

Soft shell clams, or steamers, have thin, elongated white shells and long siphons or necks extending from the shells. They are usually eaten steamed or fried.

There are many other varieties of clams that are good to eat, but their availability is often regional. Occasionally I find tiny, sweet Manila clams, no more than an inch in diameter, in my local market. Also good are razor, surf, butter, and giant geoduck (pronounced gooey-duck) clams. These and other locally available varieties can be adapted to the following recipes. Just be sure that the clams you eat were harvested in waters that are clean and certified safe by your local department of health. Buy clams (and all shellfish, for that matter) only from reputable sources.

When buying hard shell clams, look for clams that are tightly closed or that close when tapped. Hard shell clams that remain open are dead and should not be eaten. Soft shell, surf, and certain other clam varieties have shells that cannot close tightly and are very susceptible to spoilage. Touch the neck of a soft shell clam; if it is alive, it will recoil slightly. Use these clams only when they are freshly harvested.

Clams often contain sand. To eliminate it, soak the clams in cold salted water for 1 hour, changing the water once, before cooking or opening. Always scrub clams well with a stiff brush under cold running water to remove fine sand embedded in the ridges of the shells. Never keep clams covered with water or in a sealed plastic bag for long periods of time, or they will suffocate and die.

At home, keep clams in the refrigerator, covered with a damp towel that will allow air to circulate around them. Shucked clams should be kept refrigerated in a tightly sealed container embedded in a bowl of ice. Use them as soon as possible. Figure on 6 to 12 medium-size clams per serving.

You can open hard shell clams with a knife or by subjecting them to heat. Because their shells break easily, soft shell clams usually are opened by heat. If you are planning to open clams with a knife, placing them in the freezer for about 30 minutes to 1 hour causes the muscle to relax and makes them easier to shuck. Since the clams do not freeze solidly, they can be eaten raw or cooked.

Clams in the shell can be frozen for storage. Scrub them, place in plastic freezer bags, and seal tightly. Just before using, remove the clams from the freezer and rinse them in cold water. Clams that have been frozen solid should be used in recipes that call for cooking.

Shucked clams may also be frozen, and sometimes can be purchased that way.

To use, thaw frozen clams in the refrigerator overnight and cook them as soon as possible. Never refreeze clams.

Clams can be steamed, roasted, microwaved, or grilled until they open, and can be eaten immediately, or they can be subjected to further cooking in chowders or fritters or as stuffed clams on the half shell. Discard clams that refuse to open.

CHUNKY CLAM SOUP

Serves 4

¼ cup olive oil
1 large onion, diced
3 medium-size ripe tomatoes, seeded and
    chopped
2 celery stalks, thinly sliced
1 small green pepper, seeded and diced
2 garlic cloves, finely chopped
¼ teaspoon dried thyme
1 bay leaf
1 bottle (8 ounces) clam juice
2 cups water
Hot red pepper sauce
2 dozen shucked clams (1 pint) with their
    juice
1 cup small pasta (ditalini, small elbows,
    or shells)
2 tablespoons chopped fresh parsley

1. In a large pot, heat the oil over medium heat. Add the onion and sauté until tender, about 5 minutes.

2. Stir in the tomatoes, celery, green pepper, garlic, thyme, bay leaf, clam juice, water, and hot red pepper sauce to taste. Bring to a simmer.

3. Chop the clams if large. In a large pot of boiling salted water, cook the pasta until firm yet tender to the bite. Drain well and add the pasta, clams, and reserved juice to the soup. Return the soup to a simmer. Sprinkle with parsley and serve with additional hot pepper sauce.

GRILLED CLAMS

Serves 4–8

4 dozen soft or hard shell clams,
    scrubbed
Melted butter
Lemon wedges
Hot pepper sauce

1. Prepare a barbecue grill. Arrange the clams on a rack. Cook just until the shells open, about 5 to 10 minutes.

2. Serve the clams in the shells, with bowls of hot clam juice, melted butter, lemon, and hot pepper sauce.

STEAMED CLAMS

Serves 4–8

1 cup water, wine, beer, or broth
4 dozen soft or hard shell clams,
    scrubbed
Melted butter
Lemon wedges
Hot pepper sauce

"The best way to eat steamers is undoubtedly in the delectable classic fashion which gave them their name, for the clams are cooked by steaming, after which they are picked up in the fingers by the neck, dipped first into a bowl of clam broth and then into a bowl of melted butter, and popped into the mouth, where the teeth shuck the siphon out of its inedible tough black skin in the same motion in which the rest of the clam is swallowed."

Waverly Root,
Food

1. In a large pot, combine the water and clams. Cover tightly and bring to a boil. Reduce the heat and steam for 5 to 10 minutes, or until the shells open.

2. Remove the clams to a serving bowl; reserve the cooking liquid. Strain the liquid through cheesecloth or a paper coffee filter. Serve the clams in the shells, with bowls of hot clam liquid, melted butter, lemon, and hot pepper sauce, or use for stuffed clams, chowder, etc.

OLD-FASHIONED NEW ENGLAND CLAM CHOWDER

New Englanders are very serious about their creamy clam chowder, so much so that a bill was once proposed in the Maine legislature banning the use of tomatoes in clam chowder.

Serves 8

4 dozen medium to large clams, scrubbed, or 1 quart minced clams with their juice
¼ pound salt pork, diced
1 large onion, finely chopped
1½ pounds potatoes, peeled
Salt
¼ teaspoon freshly ground black pepper
2 cups milk
1 cup heavy cream
Cold butter (optional)

"On the cups of some of the shells were splotches of deep purple; Indians used to hack such splotches out of clamshells for wampum. Fresh from the coal-black mud and uncontaminated by ketchup or sauce, they were the best clams I have ever eaten."

Joseph Mitchell,
McSorley's Wonderful Saloon

1. If using shucked clams, skip to step 2. Otherwise, in a large pot, combine the unopened clams with 2 cups water. Cover and bring to a simmer over medium heat. Cook just until the clams open, about 5 minutes. Shell the clams and strain the juice through a sieve lined with a double thickness of cheesecloth or a paper coffee filter. Measure the liquid and add enough water to equal 4 cups. Chop the clams and set them aside.

2. In a large pot, cook the salt pork over medium heat until lightly browned. Stir in the onion and cook for 5 minutes, or until tender.

3. Add the potatoes, salt to taste, pepper, and reserved clam juice. Bring to a simmer and cook for 20 minutes, or until the potatoes are tender.

4. Stir in the clams, milk, and cream. Heat through but do not boil. Serve immediately, topped with a thin slice of cold butter, if desired.

CLAMS BERCY

Bercy is a section of Paris that was at one time famous as the center of the wine trade. Recipes named for this district usually contain wine and chopped shallots, but if shallots are not available, you can substitute scallions.

Serves 4

¼ cup olive oil
2 tablespoons butter
¼ cup chopped shallots
¼ cup chopped fresh parsley
3 tablespoons chopped drained capers
½ teaspoon dried thyme
¼ teaspoon freshly ground black pepper
1 cup dry white wine
4 dozen small clams, scrubbed

1. In a large pot, heat the oil and butter over medium heat. Add the shallots and cook, stirring frequently, for 2 to 3 minutes. Stir in the parsley, capers, thyme, pepper, and wine. Bring to a simmer.

2. Add the clams and cover. Cook for 5 minutes, or just until the clams open. Transfer the opened clams to a bowl and keep warm. Continue cooking the unopened clams a few minutes longer, and then discard any clams that refuse to open. Pour the sauce over the clams and serve immediately.

"The menus of Japanese wedding banquets customarily include *hamaguri*, clam broth; its role is not stimulant but symbolic—the tight closing together of the two halves of the clamshell provides a model for the union of the newly wedded couple."

Waverly Root,
Food

CLAM AND SAUSAGE CASSEROLE

This hearty casserole is wonderful with mashed potatoes.

Serves 6–8

1 pound Italian sweet sausages, cut into
    1-inch pieces
2 cups water
2 tablespoons olive oil
1 large onion, chopped
1 large green pepper, seeded and
    chopped
1 can (14½ ounces) Italian peeled
    tomatoes, chopped
1 can (8 ounces) tomato sauce
2 large garlic cloves, finely chopped
2 ounces chopped prosciutto or boiled
    ham
½ cup dry white wine
½ teaspoon sweet paprika
½ to 1 teaspoon crushed red pepper
1 bay leaf
½ teaspoon salt
4 dozen small clams, scrubbed
¼ cup chopped fresh parsley

1. Place the sausages in a medium skillet. Add the water, cover, and simmer until all of the water has evaporated. Remove the cover and brown the sausages on all sides.

2. In a large saucepan, heat the oil over medium heat. Add the onion and green pepper and sauté until very tender, about 10 minutes. Stir in the tomatoes with their juice, tomato sauce, garlic, prosciutto, wine, paprika, crushed red pepper, bay leaf, salt, and sausages. Bring to a simmer and cook for 20 minutes, or until the sauce is thick.

3. Add the clams and cover the pan. Cook until the clams open, about 5 minutes. Transfer to a large serving bowl, sprinkle with parsley, and serve.

BEER BATTER CLAM FRITTERS

Save the clam juice to use in another recipe. It freezes well.

Serves 6–8

1½ cups all-purpose flour
1 teaspoon salt
½ teaspoon baking powder
¼ teaspoon ground red pepper
2 eggs, separated
¾ cup beer
2 tablespoons melted unsalted butter
Vegetable oil for deep frying
2 dozen shucked clams, drained and
    chopped
¼ cup finely chopped onion

1. In a large bowl, combine the flour, salt, baking powder, and pepper. In a small bowl, beat the egg yolks. Gradually stir the beer, egg yolks, and butter into the dry ingredients just until moistened. The batter should be very thick and slightly lumpy. Cover and refrigerate for 4 hours or overnight.

2. In a deep fryer or heavy deep saucepan, heat the oil to 375° F.

3. Beat the egg whites until soft peaks form. Fold into the batter. Fold the clams and onion into the batter.

4. Drop the batter by tablespoonfuls into the hot oil. Do not crowd the pan. Fry for 3 to 4 minutes, or until golden brown on all sides. Remove with a slotted spoon. Drain on paper towels. Repeat with the remaining batter. Serve hot.

ROASTED CLAMS

Serves 4–8

4 dozen soft or hard shell clams,
    scrubbed
Melted butter
Lemon wedges
Hot pepper sauce

1. Preheat the oven to 450° F. Place the clams in a large roasting pan and roast for 10 to 15 minutes, or until the shells open.

2. Serve the clams in the shells, with bowls of hot clam juice, melted butter, lemon, and hot pepper sauce.

SWISS AND BACON BAKED CLAMS

Serves 4–6

4 slices bacon
1 medium onion, finely chopped
1 cup fresh bread crumbs
1 cup shredded Swiss cheese
2 tablespoons finely chopped fresh
    parsley
¼ teaspoon freshly ground black pepper
1½ dozen small clams on the half shell

1. In a medium skillet, cook the bacon over medium heat until almost crisp. Remove the bacon and reserve the drippings. Add the onion to the skillet and sauté until tender, about 5 minutes. Chop the bacon finely. Stir the bread crumbs, cheese, parsley, pepper, and bacon into the skillet.

2. Preheat the oven to 450° F. Arrange the clams on a rack in a shallow roasting pan.

3. Top each clam with a spoonful of cheese-crumb mixture. Bake for 15 minutes, or until the cheese is melted. Run the clams under the broiler, if necessary, to brown.

HAZELNUT CLAMS

Serves 4

½ cup hazelnuts
2 dozen small clams on the half shell
½ cup finely chopped fresh parsley
4 tablespoons unsalted butter
2 garlic cloves, finely chopped
¼ teaspoon freshly ground black pepper

1. Preheat the oven to 350° F. Place the hazelnuts in a small pan and bake until lightly toasted, about 10 minutes. Transfer the nuts to a kitchen towel and rub off the skins. Let cool completely. Chop the nuts finely.

2. Arrange the clams in a single layer on a rack in a shallow baking pan.

3. In a small bowl, combine the nuts, parsley, butter, garlic, and pepper. Place a spoonful of this mixture on each clam.

4. Preheat the broiler. Broil the clams until the nuts are lightly browned and the butter is melted, about 2 minutes.

CLAMS ON THE HALF SHELL

Serves 2–4

2 dozen small clams on the half shell,
    with their juice
Lemon wedges
Cocktail sauce (page 92)
Oyster crackers

Arrange the clams on serving plates on a bed of cracked ice, being careful not to lose the juice. Serve with lemon wedges and/or cocktail sauce and oyster crackers.

SPANISH SHERRIED CLAMS

In Spain, clams prepared this way are often served at tapas bars. Tapas are hors d'oeuvres served on tiny plates, accompanying glasses of dry sherry before a meal.

Serves 2

3 tablespoons olive oil
1 large onion, finely chopped
1 sweet red pepper, seeded and finely
    chopped
¼ pound smoked ham, such as
    Westphalian, cut into thin strips
2 garlic cloves, finely chopped
2 tablespoons chopped fresh parsley
Pinch of ground red pepper
⅓ cup dry sherry
2 dozen small clams, scrubbed

1. In a large pot, heat the oil over medium heat. Add the onion, sweet red pepper, and ham and cook, stirring occasionally, until the vegetables are tender, about 5 minutes.

2. Stir in the garlic, parsley, and ground red pepper. Add the sherry and clams. Cover and cook until the clams open, about 5 minutes. Discard any clams that do not open.

Crabs

"The kind of crabbing my wife likes to do is to return from an afternoon's swim or sunbathing session, open the refrigerator door, and find a generous plate of Crab Cakes all ready to cook."

Euell Gibbons,
Stalking the Blue-Eyed Scallop

There are thousands of varieties of crabs, from the tiny pea crabs that live within the shells of some mussels and oysters to giant Pacific crabs that can grow to more than 12 feet in width. All of them are good to eat.

Crabs may be sold live or cooked. Cooked crab is available whole, claws only, or shelled. Shelled or "picked" crab is very convenient, since extracting the meat from the hard, spiny shells can be a time-consuming task. On the average, 4 pounds of crabs will yield only 1 pound of meat. You will need approximately 1 pound of crabs in the shell for each serving.

When buying live crabs, make sure that they are lively and active, but be cautious when handling them, since they can nip. Wear heavy cotton or rubber work gloves. Keep the crabs in the refrigerator in a shallow tray covered with a damp towel, and cook them the same day.

Picked crabmeat is sold fresh in plastic containers or pasteurized in refrigerated cans. Both have been cooked and need no further cooking for salads and just a gentle heating for hot dishes. At home, keep crabmeat in the refrigerator. Fresh crabmeat will keep for 3 days, while pasteurized will keep for several months, provided that the seal is not broken. Once the container is opened, pasteurized crabmeat should be used within 3 days. One pound of crabmeat will serve 4 to 6, depending on the recipe.

As crabs grow, they periodically shed their outer covering. Blue crabs marketed at this stage are called soft shell crabs and are completely edible—legs, claws, and all. Usually they are fried or broiled until crisp. Soft shell crabs are at their best during the warmer months, from May through August. Buy the crabs live and clean them yourself, or have them cleaned at the fish market. Soft shells are also available cleaned and frozen. Thaw overnight in the refrigerator. Smaller crabs are thought to be sweeter and more tender. Figure on 2 or 3 soft shell crabs per serving.

To clean soft shell crabs, cut off the "mouth and face" behind the eyes with heavy kitchen shears. Turn the crab over and cut off the "apron," a flap that folds under the body. Lift the top shell and snip out the spongy gills on each side. Rinse under cold water, and pat dry with paper towels.

SPICED CRABS

Serves 4–6

12 live blue crabs
1 cup cider vinegar
2 to 3 tablespoons crab boil or Old Bay
    Seasoning
Salt
Melted butter
Lemon wedges

1. Place the crabs in the sink and rinse them with warm water.

2. In a large pot fitted with a raised rack, combine the vinegar with 1 cup water. The liquid should reach just below the level of the rack.

3. Place a layer of crabs on the rack and sprinkle them with the crab boil and salt to taste. Continue layering crabs and seasoning.

4. Cover the pot and bring the water to a simmer. Cook until the crabs turn red, about 10 minutes. Serve with melted butter and lemon wedges.

CREAM OF CRAB SOUP

Serves 4

3 tablespoons unsalted butter
1 medium onion, finely chopped
2 tablespoons all-purpose flour
2 cups water
2 cups half-and-half
1 pound crabmeat, picked over to
    remove shells and cartilage
2 tablespoons dry sherry
½ teaspoon salt
¼ teaspoon freshly ground white pepper
Pinch of ground red pepper
1 tablespoon chopped fresh parsley

1. In a large saucepan, melt the butter over medium heat. Add the onion and sauté until very tender, about 10 minutes. Add the flour and cook, stirring constantly, for about 1 minute.

2. Stir in the water and bring to a boil. Add the half-and-half and bring to a simmer. Add the crabmeat, sherry, salt, and peppers. Cook for 3 minutes longer. Sprinkle with parsley just before serving.

CRUNCHY SOFT SHELL CRABS

John Simmons makes some of the best soft shell crabs I have ever eaten. He says the secret is the cracker meal coating. When I asked him for his recipe, he was happy to share it, but since he learned it while working in a restaurant, his version makes enough to cook hundreds of crabs! Here is a scaled-down recipe.

   Stand back when frying soft shell crabs, since they have a tendency to pop and spatter.

Serves 4–6

1 cup all-purpose flour
1 teaspoon salt
¼ teaspoon ground red pepper
2 eggs
½ cup milk
12 soft shell crabs, cleaned
1 cup cracker meal
Oil for deep frying
Lemon wedges

1. On a piece of waxed paper, combine the flour, salt, and pepper. In a shallow bowl, beat the eggs and milk.

2. Lightly coat the crabs with the flour mixture, dip them in the egg mixture, then coat them with cracker meal.

3. In a deep fryer or heavy deep saucepan, heat the oil to 375° F. Fry the crabs, a few at a time, until golden brown and crisp, about 3 to 4 minutes. Drain well on paper towels. Serve with lemon wedges.

"A crabbe, breke hym a-sonder in a dysshe, make ye shelle cleane and put him in the stuffe againe; tempre it with vynegre and pouder, then cover it with brede, and send it to the kytchyn to hete; then set it to your soverayne, and breke the grete clawes, and laye them in a disshe."

Wynkyn de Worde,
Boke of Kervynge

CRAB CAKES

These are quite irresistible. They are so rich and satisfying that just 8 ounces of crabmeat makes enough to serve 4. Serve with coleslaw, tartar sauce, and French-fried potatoes.

Serves 4

½ pound crabmeat, picked over to
    remove shells and cartilage
2½ cups fresh bread crumbs
¼ cup minced celery
¼ cup minced onion
1 egg, beaten
¼ cup mayonnaise
1 teaspoon lemon juice
½ teaspoon salt
¼ teaspoon dry mustard
⅛ teaspoon ground red pepper
2 tablespoons unsalted butter
2 tablespoons vegetable oil
Tartar Sauce (page 93)

1. In a medium bowl, combine the crabmeat, 1 cup bread crumbs, celery, onion, egg, mayonnaise, lemon juice, salt, mustard, and pepper.

2. Spread the remaining bread crumbs on a sheet of waxed paper. Divide the crab mixture into 8 portions and shape each into a patty about ¾ inch thick. Coat the cakes with bread crumbs on all sides, and place them on a rack. Refrigerate for 1 hour.

3. In a large skillet, melt the butter with the oil over medium heat. Fry the crab cakes until lightly browned on both sides, about 6 to 8 minutes. Serve with tartar sauce.

"I have spent some happy evenings in Baltimore in one of those restaurants where all that is required for happiness is a pile of Maryland blue crabs on a piece of butcher paper and a wooden mallet and a supply of napkins."

Calvin Trillin,
Alice, Let's Eat

CAJUN CRAB SOUP

Oysters, clams, and mussels are also good when substituted in this main-course soup.

Serves 6

4 tablespoons unsalted butter
1 large onion, chopped
1 green pepper, seeded and chopped
1 celery stalk, chopped
2 garlic cloves, finely chopped
2 tablespoons all-purpose flour
1 bottle (8 ounces) clam juice
2 cups water
3 medium tomatoes, peeled, seeded, and
  chopped
½ cup chopped cooked ham
1 bay leaf
Hot red pepper sauce, to taste
8 ounces sliced fresh okra or 1 package
  (10 ounces) frozen cut okra
1 pound crabmeat, picked over to
  remove shells and cartilage
8 ounces small shrimp, shelled and deveined
3 cups hot cooked rice

1. In a large pot, melt the butter over medium heat. Add the onion and cook until tender, about 5 minutes. Add the green pepper, celery, and garlic and cook for an additional 5 minutes. Stir in the flour and cook for 2 minutes.

2. Stir in the clam juice, water, tomatoes, ham, bay leaf, and hot red pepper sauce. Bring to a simmer. Reduce the heat to low and cook for 30 minutes.

3. Stir in the okra and cook for 30 minutes more.

4. Add the crabmeat and shrimp. Simmer just until the shrimp turn opaque, about 5 minutes. Taste for seasoning. Ladle into serving bowls and top each one with a scoop of rice.

"The stone crab is much larger than the northern crab and has a shell harder than a landlord's heart."
Damon Runyon

CONFETTI CRAB SALAD

This salad makes a tasty sandwich filling or a spread for crackers and toast. For a more elaborate presentation, stuff the salad into avocado halves or hollowed tomatoes.

Serves 4–6

1 pound crabmeat, picked over to remove shells and cartilage
½ cup mayonnaise
½ cup finely chopped radishes
2 tablespoons finely chopped fresh parsley
2 tablespoons finely chopped onion or scallions
2 tablespoons drained capers, finely chopped
1 tablespoon lemon juice
½ teaspoon salt
⅛ teaspoon freshly ground black pepper

In a large bowl, combine all of the ingredients. Refrigerate until serving time.

SAUTEED SOFT SHELL CRABS

My husband, Charles, fondly remembers his grandmother taking him to eat sautéed soft shell crabs at Lundy's Restaurant in Brooklyn's Sheepshead Bay when he was a little boy. Lundy's served the crabs on crisp slices of toasted white bread.

Serves 3–4

½ cup all-purpose flour
½ teaspoon salt
⅛ teaspoon freshly ground black pepper
8 soft shell crabs, cleaned
4 tablespoons unsalted butter
1 tablespoon olive oil
2 tablespoons lemon juice

1. On a piece of waxed paper, combine the flour, salt, and pepper. Dust the crabs lightly with the flour mixture.

2. In a large skillet, melt the butter with the oil over medium heat. Add the crabs and cook until lightly browned, about 3 minutes on each side. Remove the crabs to a heated serving platter.

3. Stir the lemon juice into the skillet. Pour over the crabs and serve.

CRAB TACOS

When handling chilies, wear rubber gloves or slip your hands into plastic bags to prevent "burns."

Serves 6

Salsa
2 medium tomatoes, seeded and
    chopped
¼ cup finely chopped fresh coriander
¼ cup finely chopped scallions
1 small hot chili, seeded and finely
    chopped
1 garlic clove, minced
1½ tablespoons lime juice
½ teaspoon salt

4 tablespoons corn oil
¼ cup finely chopped scallions
1 pound crabmeat, picked over to
    remove shells and cartilage
1 tablespoon finely chopped fresh chili
12 taco shells, heated
1 cup shredded Monterey Jack cheese or
    cheddar
Shredded romaine lettuce

1. Combine the salsa ingredients in a serving bowl and let stand at room temperature for 1 hour.

2. In a large skillet, heat the oil over medium heat. Add the scallions and cook, while stirring, until tender, about 3 minutes. Stir in the crabmeat and cook until it is heated through, about 3 minutes. Stir in the chili.

3. Spoon the crab into hot taco shells. Top with shredded cheese and lettuce. Pass the salsa separately.

"There are three species of creatures who when they seem coming are going; when they seem going are coming: diplomats, women and crabs."

John Hay

SESAME CRAB FRITTERS

Serves 6

Dipping Sauce
½ cup soy sauce
2 tablespoons white vinegar
2 tablespoons finely chopped scallion
1 teaspoon grated fresh gingerroot

2 eggs, separated
1 cup milk
2 teaspoons Oriental sesame oil
1 cup all-purpose flour
1 tablespoon toasted sesame seeds
1 teaspoon salt
1 pound crabmeat, picked over to
    remove shells and cartilage
½ cup minced scallions
Peanut or corn oil

1. Combine the sauce ingredients in a serving bowl and set aside.

2. In a bowl, whisk together the egg yolks, milk, and sesame oil. Combine the flour, sesame seeds, and salt and stir in. Add the crabmeat and scallions.

3. In a bowl, beat the egg whites until stiff peaks form. Fold the egg whites into the crab mixture.

4. In a large, deep skillet, heat ½ inch oil over medium heat until a small drop of the crab mixture sizzles when added to it. Place heaping tablespoonfuls of the crab mixture, a few at a time, in the hot oil. Do not crowd the pan. Cook until the fritters are golden brown, about 2 minutes on each side. Remove with a slotted spoon and drain on paper towels. Repeat with the remaining batter. Serve with the dipping sauce.

CARIBBEAN DEVILED CRABS

Serves 4–6

2 tablespoons unsalted butter
¼ cup chopped scallions
1 large garlic clove, finely chopped
2 to 3 tablespoons minced green chili
1 tablespoon curry powder
1 pound crabmeat, picked over to
    remove shells and cartilage
1 cup fresh bread crumbs
¼ cup chopped fresh coriander
1 egg, lightly beaten
½ teaspoon salt
½ cup heavy cream
1 tablespoon melted unsalted butter

1. Preheat the oven to 350° F. Butter 6 large crab or scallop shells or a shallow 1-quart casserole. Arrange the shells in a shallow baking pan.

2. In a small skillet, melt the butter over moderate heat. Add the scallions, garlic, and chili. Cook, stirring frequently, for about 3 minutes, or until softened. Stir in the curry powder.

3. In a large bowl, combine the crabmeat, ¼ cup bread crumbs, coriander, egg, salt, cream, and scallion mixture. Spoon into the prepared shells or baking dish.

4. Combine the remaining bread crumbs with the melted butter, and sprinkle over the crab mixture. Bake for 25 minutes, or until the top is browned.

LOBSTERS

"And like a lobster boil'd, the morn
From black to red began to turn."

Samuel Butler,
Hudibras

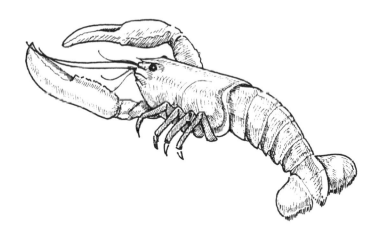

Today lobsters are synonymous with luxury, but that wasn't always the case. At one time lobsters were so cheap and plentiful that they were used as bait for cod and striped bass by New England fishermen. Not only were they abundant, some grew to enormous size. Specimens as large as 6 feet in length were found in New York waters.

Today the average lobster available in the market weighs 1 to 2 pounds, perfect for 1 to 2 servings. Larger sizes are good cut up for stews and salads.

Two kinds of lobsters are generally available, the northeastern lobster and the spiny or rock lobster. Northeastern lobsters are easily recognized by their large front claws. Usually they are sold live, but occasionally shelled, cooked meat is available.

Spiny lobsters have small front claws, though they do have meaty tails. Spiny or rock lobster tails are usually sold as frozen tails.

We tend to think of lobsters as bright red, but that is the color they turn after cooking. Live lobsters are actually a dark greenish brown. When buying fresh lobsters, look for the lively ones that move when handled. Turn the lobster on its back. If it does not react by moving its legs, it should be rejected. Always handle lobsters carefully, making sure the claws are banded together, as they can give you a nasty pinch.

Many lobster connoisseurs prefer female lobsters because of their creamy red roe. To tell a male from a female, turn the lobster on its back and look at the first pair of small fins, called swimmerets, on the tail. A female lobster's are hairy and rounded, whereas the male's are hairless and pointed.

At home a live lobster may be kept for 1 to 2 days if placed in a paper bag pierced with holes so that the lobster can breathe. Refrigerate the bag.

The simplest way to cook a live lobster is to put it headfirst into a large pot of rapidly boiling water. Follow the timing instructions for Steamed or Boiled Lobsters on page 35. For broiling or baking, kill the lobster by plunging it into boiling water. Remove it about a minute after the water returns to a boil and the lobster is limp. To cut it up, turn the lobster on its back on a cutting board. With a large knife or heavy kitchen shears, split the lobster in half lengthwise. Remove the beige sand sac from the head and the vein in the tail. Cut the lobster into pieces or remove the meat from the shells, according to the recipe. A 1¼-pound lobster yields about 4 ounces of shelled meat.

Lobster shells can be made into a delicious broth to use as a substitute for clam juice in many recipes. Just chop up the leftover shells and throw them into a pot with a chopped onion, celery stalk, and carrot and cold water to cover. Bring to a simmer and cook for 45 minutes. Strain the liquid and refrigerate or freeze it for later use.

STEAMED OR BOILED LOBSTERS

Many cooks prefer to steam lobsters because they don't become saturated with water, as when they are boiled. Don't try to cook more than two lobsters in one pot unless you are using a really large vessel, such as a washboiler.

Serves 2

2 live lobsters (about 1¼ to 1½ pounds each)
Salt

1. To steam the lobsters, place a rack in an 8-quart or larger pot. Add enough water to reach just below the rack and bring it to a boil. To boil the lobsters, fill an 8-quart or larger pot with cold water and bring to a boil. Add salt to taste.

2. Plunge the lobsters headfirst into the pot and cover. As soon as the water returns to a boil and steam begins to escape, time the lobsters; cook a 1¼ pound lobster 10 minutes, a 1½ pound lobster 12 minutes. (Larger lobsters—1¾ to 2 pounds—need 15 to 18 minutes.)

3. With tongs, remove the lobsters to a cutting board. Drain boiled lobsters by plunging a heavy knife into each head. Hold the lobsters by the tail to drain out the water. Serve hot or cold.

HOW TO EAT A LOBSTER

A whole, cooked lobster looks formidable, but all you need to enjoy it is a little patience. To simplify matters, have on hand nut or shellfish crackers and small forks. Provide empty plates to collect the shells. Many restaurants have large bibs for lobster eaters, and that certainly can be a good idea, though extra napkins will do as well.

Everything inside the lobster is edible except for the small sac just inside the head, the yellowish, feathery gills lining the chest cavity, and the vein inside the tail. The green tomalley is delicious, as is the red or coral-colored roe found in female lobsters. The roe can be removed and blended with melted butter and lemon juice for a quick sauce for the lobster.

To eat, twist off the large claws of northeastern lobsters and crack them in several places with a nut or seafood cracker. Extract the meat with the aid of a small oyster fork. Break off the legs and suck out the meat and juices.

Separate the tail from the chest cavity by twisting the lobster with your hands. The chest cavity contains the tomalley, the roe, and morsels of meat in the crevices behind the gills. Pull the tail meat out from the shell with a fork, then cut it into bite-size pieces.

LOBSTER CHOWDER

Lobster chowder is a real luxury. You can double the value of a couple of lobsters by using the meat in a salad, then simmering the shells for chowder. Other shellfish, or even mild fish fillets, could substitute for the lobster meat.

Serves 6

10 cups water
2 live lobsters (about 1¼ to 1½ pounds each)
1 teaspoon salt
4 ears of corn or 2 packages (10 ounces each) frozen corn kernels, thawed
1 large onion, quartered
1 bay leaf
4 sprigs fresh thyme or ½ teaspoon dried
½ teaspoon black peppercorns
1 teaspoon dried tarragon
4 medium red new potatoes, diced
1 large leek, thinly sliced
Freshly ground white pepper to taste
1 cup heavy cream

1. In a large pot, bring the water to a boil. Add the lobsters and salt. Cover and cook for 10 minutes. Remove the lobsters and let them cool. Reserve the cooking liquid.

2. When the lobsters are cool enough to handle, remove the meat, reserving the shells. Cut the meat into small pieces. Cover and refrigerate. Put the lobster shells in the pot with the cooking liquid.

3. If using fresh corn, cut and scrape kernels from the cobs with a knife. Set the kernels aside. Add the corn cobs to the lobster cooking liquid, along with the onion, bay leaf, thyme, and peppercorns. Bring to a simmer. Cook for 1 hour. Strain the liquid through a fine strainer and discard the solids. There should be about 8 cups of liquid.

4. Bring the liquid back to a simmer. Add the tarragon, potatoes, leek, and white pepper. Cook for 20 minutes, or until the potatoes are tender. Add the lobster meat, corn, and cream. Return to a simmer. Taste for seasoning and serve hot.

"He takes a lobster apart the way a senior infantry sergeant disassembles an exceedingly complicated machine gun...."

Calvin Trillin,
Alice, Let's Eat

LOBSTER RAGOUT

Delicate, anise-flavored chervil tastes wonderful with lobster. If it is not available, substitute tarragon or chives.

Serves 2–3

1 cup dry white wine
1 teaspoon black peppercorns
1 teaspoon fennel seeds
1 tablespoon dillseed
1 bottle (8 ounces) clam juice
1 cup water
1 large live lobster (about 2 pounds)
2 tablespoons unsalted butter
2 medium carrots, peeled and cut into
    matchstick strips
1 small leek, thinly sliced
1 celery stalk, cut into matchstick strips
1 cup heavy cream
2 tablespoons chopped fresh chervil
Salt
Freshly ground white pepper

1. Bring the wine, peppercorns, fennel, dill, clam juice, and water to a boil. Lower the heat and simmer for 15 minutes. Add the lobster, cover, and cook for 15 to 18 minutes after the water returns to a boil.

2. Remove the lobster and allow to cool. Strain the cooking juices through dampened cheesecloth into a small saucepan; discard the solids. There should be about 2 cups of liquid.

3. Remove the lobster meat from the shell and cut the meat into bite-size pieces. With a spoon, remove the green tomalley and red roe, if any, and set aside.

4. In a medium skillet, melt the butter and sauté the vegetables for 5 minutes. Stir in the lobster liquid. Bring to a simmer and cook until the liquid is reduced to ½ cup. Add the cream and simmer until thickened, about 2 minutes more. Stir in the lobster meat, tomalley, roe, and chervil. Season to taste with salt and pepper.

" 'Tis the voice of the lobster; I heard him declare
You have baked me too brown, I must sugar my hair."
Lewis Carroll,
Through the Looking-Glass

LOBSTER AND ORANGE SALAD

Serves 2

1 lobster (2 pounds), cooked and cooled
    (about 2 cups meat)
1 navel orange
⅓ to ½ cup mayonnaise
2 tablespoons finely chopped fresh basil
    or ½ teaspoon dried
2 teaspoons lemon juice
Salt
Freshly ground white pepper
1 small ripe avocado
Tender lettuce leaves

1. Remove the lobster meat from the shell. Place the tomalley and roe, if any, in a large bowl. Cut the meat into bite-size pieces.

2. Grate ½ teaspoon orange zest (colored part only). Combine the zest with the tomalley, roe, mayonnaise, basil, lemon juice, and salt and pepper to taste. Stir in the lobster meat. Cover and refrigerate until ready to serve.

3. Peel the avocado and cut into bite-size pieces. Toss the avocado with the lobster. Peel the orange and cut into sections.

4. Arrange the lettuce on 2 plates. Top with the lobster mixture, garnish with orange sections, and serve immediately.

LOBSTER CLUB SANDWICHES

The ultimate club sandwich.

Serves 2

2 cups diced cooked lobster meat
¼ cup finely chopped scallions
⅓ cup mayonnaise, preferably
    homemade
2 teaspoons lemon juice
½ teaspoon salt
Freshly ground white pepper
6 slices toasted brioche or egg bread
6 slices bacon, crisply cooked and halved
1 large tomato, thinly sliced
6 Boston lettuce leaves

1. In a bowl, combine the lobster, scallions, mayonnaise, lemon juice, salt, and pepper to taste.

2. Spread half of the lobster salad on 2 slices of toast. Top with half of the bacon, tomato, and lettuce. Make a second layer of toast, lobster salad, bacon, tomato, and lettuce and place over the first. Top with the remaining toast. Cut the sandwiches in half diagonally and secure with sandwich picks.

FETTUCCINE with LOBSTER SAUCE

Serves 4–6

1 live lobster (about 2 pounds)
⅓ cup olive oil
1 can (35 ounces) Italian peeled
    tomatoes, chopped
2 garlic cloves, minced
¼ cup chopped fresh parsley
1 tablespoon chopped fresh basil or 1
    teaspoon dried
1 teaspoon salt
½ teaspoon crushed red pepper
½ teaspoon oregano
¼ teaspoon freshly ground black pepper
1 pound fettuccine

"All the ingenious men and all the scientific men, and all the imaginative men in the world could never invent, if all their wits were broiled into one, anything so curious and so ridiculous as a lobster."

Charles Kingsley,
The Water Babies

1. Bring a large pot of water to a boil. Plunge the lobster headfirst into the water. Cover, bring the water back to a boil, and cook for 5 minutes. With tongs, remove the lobster and drain it well. Set aside to cool.

2. When cool enough to handle, twist off the lobster tail and claws from body. Scoop the green tomalley and red roe, if any, into a small bowl. Crack the claws and remove the meat from the claws and tails. Reserve the shells. Cut the meat into ½-inch pieces. Cover and refrigerate the meat, tomalley, and roe.

3. In a large saucepan, heat the oil over medium heat. Add the lobster shells and cook, stirring frequently, for 3 minutes. Stir in the tomatoes with their juice, garlic, 2 tablespoons parsley, basil, salt, red pepper, oregano, and black pepper. Bring to a simmer and cook, stirring occasionally, for 45 minutes, or until the sauce is thickened.

4. With a slotted spoon, remove the lobster shells. Stir in the lobster meat, tomalley, and roe. Simmer for 2 to 3 minutes, or until heated through.

5. Cook the fettuccine in boiling salted water until firm, yet tender to the bite. Drain the pasta well. Transfer to a heated serving bowl. Top with the lobster sauce and stir well. Sprinkle with the remaining parsley.

MICROWAVE LOBSTER TAILS with HERB BUTTER

Serves 4

½ cup (1 stick) unsalted butter
4 lobster tails (about 8 ounces each),
    thawed if frozen
3 tablespoons chopped assorted fresh
    herbs, such as tarragon, parsley,
    chives, basil, thyme
Freshly ground black pepper to taste
Lemon wedges

1. Place the butter in a small microwave-safe bowl. Cover and microwave on high for 45 seconds, or until melted.

2. Arrange the lobster tails around the outer edges of a microwave-safe dish. Brush with melted butter. Cover the dish with plastic wrap, turning one corner up to vent. Microwave on high for 6 to 8 minutes, or until the lobster meat becomes opaque.

3. Stir the herbs and pepper into the remaining butter. Serve the lobster tails with the herb butter and lemon wedges.

BAKED STUFFED LOBSTER TAILS

Serves 4

4 lobster tails (6–8 ounces each), thawed
    if frozen
4 tablespoons melted unsalted butter
1 cup soft fresh bread crumbs
1 teaspoon dried tarragon
1 teaspoon salt
¼ teaspoon freshly ground black pepper
Lemon wedges

1. Preheat the oven to 450° F. With scissors, remove the thin shell covering the underside of the tail by cutting along each side.

2. In a small bowl, combine 2 tablespoons melted butter, bread crumbs, tarragon, salt, and pepper. Spoon the bread crumb mixture over the lobster tails. Drizzle with the remaining butter.

3. Place the lobster tails in a baking pan. Bake for 20 minutes, or until the lobster meat is opaque and the crumbs are browned. Serve with lemon wedges.

GRILLED LOBSTERS with VANILLA BUTTER

The vanilla butter really enhances the sweet fresh flavor of the lobster, but the herb butter on page 40 is also delicious. In fact, you might like to serve both. Accompany the lobsters with a rich California Chardonnay.

Serves 2

Vanilla Butter
½ cup (1 stick) unsalted butter
Pinch of salt
4 drops vanilla extract

2 live lobsters (about 1¼ pounds each)
2 tablespoons corn oil
Lemon wedges

1. In a small saucepan, melt the butter over low heat. Add the salt and vanilla. Remove the butter from the heat and keep warm while preparing the lobsters.

2. Prepare the grill. Bring a large pot of salted water to a boil. Plunge the lobsters headfirst into the water. Cook for 1 minute, or until limp. Place the lobsters on a cutting board and split them in half lengthwise. With the blunt side of the knife, crack the claws. Brush the cut sides of the lobsters with oil.

3. Place the lobsters on the grill, shell side down. Cook for 4 to 5 minutes. Turn the lobsters and cook for 3 minutes longer, or until the shells are bright red and the meat is no longer translucent. Serve immediately with the vanilla butter and lemon wedges.

"Lobster! I have eaten it in many countries but nowhere has it surpassed, or even equaled, the lobster of New England."

Waverly Root,
"An Epicure's Memoirs of a New England Boyhood"

LOBSTER IN CHAMPAGNE VINAIGRETTE

It's important to use a good-quality mild vinegar in this recipe. White wine, tarragon, or raspberry vinegar may be substituted for the Champagne vinegar.

Serves 4

Champagne Vinaigrette
3 tablespoons Champagne vinegar
1 tablespoon lemon juice
¼ teaspoon salt
⅛ teaspoon ground red pepper
⅔ cup olive oil
1 tablespoon finely chopped fresh basil
1 tablespoon snipped fresh chives

4 live lobsters (about 1¼ pounds each)
¼ cup fresh bread crumbs
Lemon wedges

1. In a small bowl, whisk together the vinegar, lemon juice, salt, and pepper. Gradually whisk in the oil. Stir in the basil and chives. Set aside.

2. Bring a large pot of salted water to a boil. Plunge the lobsters headfirst into the water. Cook for 1 minute, or until limp. Place the lobsters on a cutting board and split them in half lengthwise. With the blunt side of the knife, crack the claws.

3. Preheat the broiler. Arrange the lobsters cut side up on a broiling pan. Spoon some of the vinaigrette on each lobster half. Sprinkle with the bread crumbs. Broil the lobsters about 4 to 5 inches from the heat until the crumbs are browned and the lobster meat is opaque, about 10 minutes. Serve with lemon wedges.

MUSSELS

"... to this day the first food I ask for when I land in France is a dish of mussels. Before embarking on the ferry to return home I always try to go to a restaurant where I know there will be mussels, sweet, small mussels, so small in fact that you get about seventy or eighty to a portion...."

Elizabeth David,
An Omelette and a Glass of Wine

Beautiful, blue-black mussels have a lot going for them. Not only do they look and taste great, they are one of the most inexpensive shellfish you can buy. Mussels may be gathered wild, but more are being cultivated on mussel farms. Farmed mussels differ from their wild counterparts in that they are cleaner and less likely to contain sand. Usually they have thinner, lighter shells, so you get more mussels to the pound.

Mussels breathe when out of the water by opening and closing their shells. When buying mussels, look for shells that are tightly closed. To test "gapers," tap them with your fingers or run very cold water over them; they should begin to close. Discard any mussels that refuse to close, and those with cracked or broken shells. Mussels that feel light are probably empty, and those that are too heavy for their size are probably full of sand and should also be discarded. Occasionally a mussel will contain a tiny crab, called a chowder or pea crab. These crabs are completely edible and are considered in some cultures to be a delicacy.

To store mussels at home, place them in a shallow layer on a flat tray, so that the mussels are able to breathe. Cover them with a damp towel and refrigerate until ready to use. Mussels take well to steaming, baking, and even grilling. To prepare the mussels for cooking, rinse them well and soak them in cold water for 5 minutes. Scrub them with a stiff brush and scrape off any seaweed or barnacles. The beards, fine threads that mussels use to anchor themselves to rocks or pilings, should be removed. With your fingers, pull the threads from the narrow end to the broader end.

BASIC STEAMED MUSSELS

This is the cooking method for serving many types of mussel dishes. Once they are steamed, the mussels can be served hot or cold, plain or with a variety of sauces, such as Fresh Tomato Salsa (page 93) or Remoulade Sauce (page 93). These mussels may also be used as a component of other recipes, such as Mediterranean Mussel and Potato Salad (page 48) or Greek-Style Stuffed Mussels (page 47).

Serves 2–4

2 pounds mussels, scrubbed and beards removed
¼ cup dry white wine, beer, clam broth, or water
1 bay leaf

In a large pot, combine the mussels, wine, and bay leaf. Cover and cook for 4 to 5 minutes, or until the mussels open. Remove the opened mussels with a slotted spoon. Cook unopened mussels a little longer, then discard any that don't open.

MUSSELS PARISIENNE

Serves 4

¼ cup olive oil
1 large onion, chopped
2 medium tomatoes, peeled, seeded, and chopped
2 large garlic cloves, chopped
½ teaspoon dried thyme
1 bay leaf
Pinch of crumbled saffron
Pinch of ground red pepper
2 cups dry white wine
4 pounds mussels, scrubbed and beards removed
2 tablespoons chopped fresh parsley

1. In a large pot, heat the oil. Add the onion and sauté for 5 minutes. Stir in the tomatoes, garlic, thyme, bay leaf, saffron, and red pepper. Add the wine and bring to a simmer.

2. Add the mussels, cover, and cook for 5 minutes, or until the mussels open. Transfer to a large bowl and sprinkle with parsley. Serve immediately.

MUSSELS with HERBS AND CREAM

Serves 4

1½ cups dry white wine
¼ cup minced shallots
4 pounds mussels, scrubbed and beards
    removed
2 tablespoons lemon juice
1 cup heavy cream
¼ cup minced fresh herbs, such as
    parsley, tarragon, basil, dill
2 tablespoons unsalted butter
Pinch of white pepper

1. In a large pot, bring the wine and shallots to a simmer. Add the mussels. Cover and cook for 3 to 5 minutes, or until the mussels open. With a slotted spoon, transfer the opened mussels to a serving dish. Cook unopened mussels a little longer, and then discard any that refuse to open.

2. Add the lemon juice to the pot. Boil until the liquid is reduced to about half its original amount. Add the cream and cook for 2 to 3 minutes, or until slightly thickened. Stir in the herbs, butter, and pepper. Pour over the mussels and serve immediately.

MUSSELS ALLA BIANCA

Toss the mussels and their cooking juices with some spaghetti, or serve them in a bowl over slices of toasted French bread. Small clams are also good prepared this way.

Serves 2–4

⅓ cup olive oil
4 cloves garlic, finely chopped
½ teaspoon crushed red pepper
⅓ cup finely chopped fresh parsley
½ cup dry white wine
2 pounds mussels, scrubbed and beards
    removed

1. In a large pot, heat the oil over medium heat. Stir in the garlic, pepper, and parsley. Add the wine and mussels. Cover tightly and cook for 4 to 5 minutes, or until the mussels open, shaking the pan occasionally.

2. Remove the opened mussels from the pan with a slotted spoon. Continue cooking the unopened mussels a few minutes longer and then discard any that do not open. Pour the juices over the mussels and serve.

GREEK-STYLE STUFFED MUSSELS

Whole mussels stuffed with flavored rice are great on a buffet.

Serves 6

24 mussels (about 2 pounds), scrubbed
    and beards removed
1 cup dry white wine
¼ cup olive oil
1 large onion, finely chopped
½ cup long-grain rice
¼ teaspoon thyme
¼ teaspoon salt
⅛ teaspoon freshly ground black pepper
Pinch of ground cinnamon
½ cup toasted pine nuts
¼ cup dried currants
2 scallions, finely chopped

1. In a large pot, combine the mussels and wine. Cover and cook until the mussels open, about 3 to 5 minutes. Drain the liquid into a measuring cup and add enough water to equal 1¼ cups. Remove the mussels from the shells. Reserve the shells.

2. In a large saucepan, heat the oil. Add the onion and sauté for 10 minutes. Add the rice. Cook, stirring constantly, for 2 minutes. Add the reserved liquid and bring to a simmer. Stir in the thyme, salt, pepper, and cinnamon. Cover and cook for 20 minutes, or until the rice is tender. Stir in the nuts, currants, scallions, and mussels. Pack the rice mixture into the shells, including a mussel in each. Serve warm or at room temperature.

MEDITERRANEAN MUSSEL AND POTATO SALAD

Serves 4

Dressing
1 tablespoon lemon juice
1 tablespoon white wine vinegar
2 teaspoons Dijon mustard
1 garlic clove, minced
Salt
¼ teaspoon freshly ground black pepper
¼ cup olive oil
1½ pounds new potatoes, scrubbed
1 teaspoon salt
½ cup imported black olives, such as
 Kalamata, pitted and sliced
2 scallions, finely chopped
2 tablespoons chopped fresh parsley
1 tablespoon chopped drained capers
3 tablespoons dry white wine
3 pounds cooked mussels (see Basic
 Steamed Mussels, page 45)
Lettuce leaves
2 tomatoes, quartered

1. In a small bowl, whisk together the lemon juice, vinegar, mustard, garlic, salt to taste, and pepper. Gradually beat in the oil.

2. Place the potatoes in a large saucepan with cold water to cover and the salt. Cover the pan and bring to a boil over medium heat. Cook until the potatoes are tender when pierced with a knife, about 20 minutes. Drain the potatoes well and cut them into thick slices. Place the potatoes in a bowl and toss with the olives, scallions, parsley, capers, and wine. Stir in half of the dressing. Cover and chill until serving time.

3. Remove the mussels from the shells and toss the mussels with the remaining dressing. Cover and chill until serving time.

4. Arrange the lettuce leaves on a large serving platter. Combine the potatoes and mussels. Spoon onto lettuce leaves. Garnish with tomatoes.

ORIENTAL MUSSELS

Clams and oysters are also good prepared this way.

Serves 6–8

2 tablespoons vegetable oil
1 large sweet onion, thinly sliced
1 garlic clove, finely chopped
1 tablespoon fermented black beans
(available in Oriental markets),
rinsed under hot water and drained
1 tablespoon finely chopped fresh
gingerroot
4 pounds mussels, scrubbed and beards
removed
1 cup water
1 tablespoon soy sauce
½ cup finely chopped fresh coriander

1. In a large pot, heat the oil. Add the onion and sauté for 3 minutes, or just until softened. Stir in the garlic, black beans, and ginger. Cook for 1 minute more.

2. Add the mussels, water, and soy sauce to the pot. Cover and steam until the mussels open, about 3 to 5 minutes. With a slotted spoon, transfer the opened mussels to a serving dish. Continue cooking the unopened mussels for a few minutes more, and then discard any that refuse to open. Pour the liquid over the mussels and sprinkle with coriander. Serve immediately.

"In Dublin's fair city, where girls are so pretty,
I first set my eyes on sweet Molly Malone,
As she wheeled her wheelbarrow through streets broad and narrow,
Crying, Cockles and mussels! alive, alive oh!"

Folk Song

MUSSELS JAMBALAYA

Serves 4

3 pounds mussels, scrubbed and beards
    removed
2 cups dry white wine
2 tablespoons butter
2 tablespoons olive oil
1 large onion, finely chopped
2 celery stalks, thinly sliced
1 green pepper, seeded and chopped
1½ cups long-grain rice
1 can (14½ ounces) Italian peeled
    tomatoes
1 cup chopped cooked ham
2 large garlic cloves, finely chopped
1 bay leaf
½ teaspoon dried thyme
5 to 6 drops hot red pepper sauce
¼ cup chopped fresh parsley

1. In a large pot, combine the mussels and wine. Cover and cook just until the mussels open, about 3 to 5 minutes. Transfer the opened mussels to a bowl. Continue cooking unopened mussels a little longer, then discard any that do not open. Strain the cooking liquid into a measuring cup. Combine with enough water to equal 2½ cups.

2. In a large pot, heat the butter and oil over medium heat. Add the onion and sauté for 5 minutes, stirring occasionally. Stir in the celery and green pepper and cook for 5 minutes more. Add the rice and stir well.

3. Stir in the reserved cooking liquid, tomatoes with their juice, ham, garlic, bay leaf, thyme, and hot red pepper sauce. Cover and cook for 15 to 20 minutes, or until the rice is tender and the liquid is absorbed. Remove the mussels from their shells and stir in just to heat through. Spoon the jambalaya into a serving dish and sprinkle with parsley.

GARLIC BAKED MUSSELS

These mussels can be filled in advance and baked just before serving. They are good as an appetizer with French bread or as a main dish with noodles.

Serves 2–4

½ cup (1 stick) unsalted butter, softened
2 large garlic cloves, finely chopped
2 scallions, minced
2 tablespoons finely chopped fresh
    parsley
¼ teaspoon thyme
½ teaspoon salt
¼ teaspoon freshly ground black pepper
2 pounds cooked mussels (see Basic
    Steamed Mussels, page 45)

1. Preheat the oven to 450° F.

2. In a small bowl, beat together the butter, garlic, scallions, parsley, thyme, salt, and pepper.

3. Remove the top shells from the steamed mussels. Spread the mussels with the prepared butter. Arrange them on a rack in a shallow baking pan. Bake the mussels for 5 minutes, or until the butter is melted. Serve immediately.

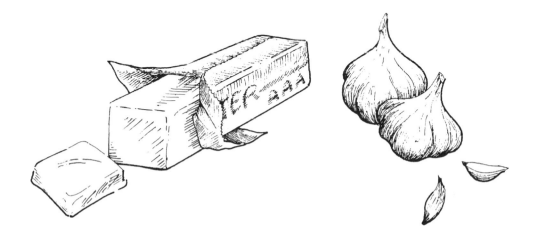

LINGUINE with MUSSEL SAUCE

Here is another recipe that works well with clams.

Serves 4–6

¼ cup olive oil
3 garlic cloves, finely chopped
¼ cup chopped fresh parsley
¼ teaspoon crushed red pepper
1 can (28 ounces) Italian peeled
    tomatoes, finely chopped
3 pounds mussels, scrubbed and beards
    removed
Salt
1 pound linguine

1. In a large pot, heat the oil over medium heat. Add the garlic and cook for 30 seconds. Stir in the parsley and red pepper. Add the tomatoes with their juice and the mussels. Cover and cook for 5 minutes, or until the mussels open. With a slotted spoon, transfer the mussels to a bowl.

2. Simmer the sauce uncovered, stirring occasionally, until thickened, about 20 minutes. Add salt to taste.

3. Remove the mussels from the shells. When the sauce is ready, stir in the mussels.

4. Meanwhile, in a large pot of boiling salted water, cook the linguine until firm yet tender to the bite. Drain the pasta well and toss with mussel sauce.

Oysters

"He was a bold man that first ate an oyster."

Jonathan Swift

Oysters might just be everybody's favorite shellfish. They come in all kinds of shapes and sizes, from the enormous half-pound Long Island Box oysters to tiny, briny Olympias from Washington State. The flavors vary almost as much as the size, depending upon where the oysters are harvested. Oysters are delicious raw but also lend themselves well to all kinds of cooking.

An old wives' tale lingers on that oysters should be eaten only in months with an *r*, but that simply is not true. The story probably got started because oysters generally spawn during the spring and summer. This causes them to become somewhat watery and a bit less flavorful. They are perfectly safe to eat, however. Warm weather also increases the danger of spoilage, but with modern refrigeration techniques this is not the problem that it once was.

Oysters have rough, craggy, paisley-shaped shells. One half, the top shell, is flat, while the lower shell is rounded and bowl-shaped, to contain the oyster and its juice. When buying oysters, look for tightly closed, unbroken shells. Once opened, the oysters should have a clean, fresh ocean scent.

Many chefs say that they can detect a fresh oyster by tapping the shell with a knife. A fresh oyster will sound solid, whereas a dead oyster will make a hollow sound and should be discarded.

Oysters are also available shucked, either fresh or frozen. Shucked oysters are sold in half-pint or pint containers. They should appear plump and creamy, and the liquid surrounding them should be clear. Shucked oysters should be kept covered in the refrigerator, preferably in a container on a bed of ice.

Oysters in the shell should be well chilled. Place them rounded side down in a single layer in a shallow pan and cover them with damp towels before refrigerating. Oysters will suffocate if kept in water or a tightly sealed container.

Opening oysters is not difficult, but it does require some practice. First, scrub the oysters with a stiff brush under cold running water.

Protect your hand with a heavy cotton glove or a thick potholder. Work over a bowl to catch the oyster liquid. Place an oyster in the protected hand, rounded shell down and with the hinge end of the shell near the base of your fingers. Hold the oyster knife in the other hand. Poke the knife tip between the two shells wherever you can find an opening. Wiggle the knife, pushing it deeper into the shell until the shell opens slightly.

Detach the oyster from its shell by cutting the muscle that connects the top shell to the oyster. Cut carefully to avoid slicing into the oyster. Pry the two shells open completely. Sever the oyster from the bottom shell by cutting the muscle near the hinge, being careful not to lose any of the oyster liquor. Twist off top shell if serving on the half shell.

Oysters also can be opened by steaming, roasting, grilling, or microwaving.

JOHN'S OYSTER STEW

John Simmons imports and wholesales fish and is a walking encyclopedia of seafood information. He says that the secret to making a good oyster stew is to heat the milk and cream separately from the oysters and their juice.

Serves 2

1 cup milk
1 cup heavy cream
2 tablespoons unsalted butter
1 pint shucked oysters with their juice
Salt
Freshly ground black pepper

1. In a small saucepan, heat the milk and cream until bubbles form around the edge.

2. In another saucepan, melt the butter over medium-low heat. Add the oysters and their juice and heat just until the oysters begin to curl around the edges. Pour the hot milk mixture and oysters simultaneously into heated soup bowls. Season to taste with salt and pepper.

"... secret and self-contained, and solitary as an oyster."

Charles Dickens,
A Christmas Carol

THE HISTORICAL OYSTER

More than any other shellfish, oysters have a place in human history. Over two thousand years ago, the Romans first tasted oysters when they visited what is now Great Britain. They liked them so much that they shipped them back to Rome in barrels packed with seaweed. Later they developed a technique for cultivating oysters closer to home to ensure a good supply.

In North America, oysters were abundant and helped the early settlers survive the long winters. In Britain, as elsewhere, they were so cheap that Charles Dickens wrote: "Poverty and oysters always seem to go together." Bartenders gave the salty oysters away free to their customers to encourage their thirst and cause them to drink more.

Some people become passionate about oysters. Perhaps for that reason, oysters have developed a reputation as an aphrodisiac. Casanova, the famous Italian lover, claimed that oysters were the key to his great success with the ladies, and ate dozens of them every evening!

CREAM OF OYSTER AND TOMATO SOUP

The base for this soup can be prepared a day ahead. Reheat gently and stir in the oysters just before serving.

Serves 4

2 tablespoons unsalted butter
½ cup chopped scallions
1 large garlic clove, finely chopped
2 medium ripe tomatoes, peeled, seeded, and chopped
2 tablespoons finely chopped fresh basil
½ teaspoon dried thyme
½ teaspoon salt
Freshly ground white pepper
1 pint shucked oysters (about 18 oysters)
2 cups heavy cream
Fresh basil leaves

1. In a medium saucepan, melt the butter over medium heat. Add the scallions and cook, stirring occasionally, until tender, about 4 minutes. Stir in the garlic. Add the tomatoes and cook until thickened, about 10 minutes. Stir in the herbs, salt, and pepper to taste.

2. Drain the oyster liquid into the pan. Add the cream and bring to a simmer. Add the oysters and cook for 2 minutes, or until they are plump. Ladle into bowls and garnish with basil leaves.

BAKED OYSTERS

Serves 2

½ cup fresh bread crumbs
¼ cup chopped fresh parsley
1 garlic clove, finely chopped, or 2 tablespoons minced shallot
Freshly ground black pepper
2 tablespoons melted butter
1 dozen oysters on the half shell

1. Preheat the oven to 400° F. In a small bowl, combine the bread crumbs, parsley, garlic, pepper to taste, and butter.

2. Arrange the oysters on a rack or a bed of coarse salt in a shallow pan. Spoon some of the bread crumb mixture over each oyster. Bake for 8 to 10 minutes, until the oysters are plump and the crumbs are browned.

OYSTER AND BACON SANDWICHES

In New Orleans, a fried oyster sandwich is called "La Médiatrice," the mediator. Husbands traditionally brought them home as a peace offering for their wives after a late night on the town.

Serves 2

¼ cup cracker meal
½ teaspoon salt
¼ teaspoon ground red pepper
¼ pound sliced bacon
8 ounces shucked oysters, drained
3 tablespoons mayonnaise
1 tablespoon prepared horseradish
2 crisp sandwich rolls, split
1 medium tomato, thinly sliced

1. On a piece of waxed paper, combine the cracker meal, salt, and pepper.

2. In a medium skillet, fry the bacon until crisp and browned. Remove the bacon and drain on paper towels. Spoon off all but 2 tablespoons of bacon fat.

3. Dip the oysters in the cracker meal mixture and shake off any excess. Heat the reserved bacon fat over medium heat and sauté the oysters until browned on all sides, about 5 minutes.

4. Combine the mayonnaise and horseradish, and spread on the rolls. Fill the rolls with the oysters, bacon, and tomato slices.

"Let's sing a song of glory to Themistocles O'Shea,
Who ate a dozen oysters on the second day of May."
Stoddard King,
The Man Who Dared

PEPPERED OYSTER SALAD

Serves 3–4

12 shucked oysters, juice reserved
½ cup olive oil
2 tablespoons fresh lime or lemon juice
¼ cup chopped green pepper
¼ cup chopped red pepper
¼ cup chopped yellow pepper
1 scallion, finely chopped
1 small garlic clove, minced
1 teaspoon Dijon mustard
1 tablespoon chopped fresh parsley
1 teaspoon chopped fresh dill
¼ teaspoon crumbled dried rosemary
Salt
Freshly ground black pepper
Radicchio and endive leaves

1. In a small saucepan, combine the oysters and their juice. Cook over medium-low heat just until the edges curl, about 2 minutes.

2. In a bowl, whisk together the oil, lime juice, chopped peppers, scallion, garlic, mustard, parsley, dill, rosemary, and salt and pepper to taste. Stir in the oysters. Cover and refrigerate for 4 hours or overnight.

3. Arrange the radicchio and endive on serving plates. Top with the oyster salad.

GINGERED OYSTERS

Serves 2–4

1 dozen oysters on the half shell
4 tablespoons butter
1 tablespoon minced fresh gingerroot
1 stalk celery, cut into 2-inch matchstick strips
2 carrots, cut into 2-inch matchstick strips
¼ teaspoon salt
Freshly ground black pepper

1. Preheat the oven to 400° F. Place a rack in a shallow roasting pan and arrange the oysters on the rack.

2. In a medium skillet, melt the butter over medium heat. Add the ginger and sauté for 1 minute. Add the celery and carrots and sauté for 4 to 5 minutes, or until tender. Stir in the salt and pepper to taste.

3. Spoon some of the vegetables over each oyster. Bake for 8 to 10 minutes, or until the oysters are plump and heated through.

OYSTERS MIGNONETTE

Many oyster connoisseurs prefer their oysters unadorned or with a simple mignonette sauce. A good white wine vinegar can be substituted for the Champagne vinegar.

Serves 4

Mignonette Sauce
¼ cup minced shallots
½ teaspoon cracked black pepper
½ cup dry white wine
½ cup Champagne vinegar

2 dozen oysters on the half shell
Crushed ice
Lemon wedges

1. In a small bowl, combine the sauce ingredients, and allow the sauce to stand at room temperature for 1 hour.

2. Arrange the oysters on individual serving plates covered with crushed ice. Serve with lemon wedges and mignonette sauce.

" 'A loaf of bread,' the Walrus said,
'Is what we chiefly need:
Pepper and vinegar besides
Are very good indeed—
Now if you're ready, Oysters dear,
We can begin to feed.'
But answer there came none—
And this was scarcely odd because
They'd eaten every one."

Lewis Carroll,
Through the Looking-Glass

GLAZED OYSTERS

For a variation, lightly sprinkle each oyster with grated Parmesan cheese before broiling.

Serves 2–4

1 cup dry white wine
2 tablespoons chopped shallots or scallions
½ cup heavy cream
1 egg yolk
¼ teaspoon salt
Freshly ground white pepper
1 dozen oysters on the half shell

1. In a small saucepan, bring the wine and shallots to a boil. Cook over medium-high heat until the liquid is reduced to ¼ cup. Add the heavy cream and boil until the liquid is reduced to ½ cup. Remove from the heat.

2. In a small bowl, beat the egg yolk with 2 tablespoons of the wine-cream reduction. Stir this into the remaining wine-cream mixture. Cook over low heat, stirring constantly, until the sauce is slightly thickened. Do not boil. Remove from the heat. Stir in the salt and pepper to taste.

3. Preheat the broiler. To prevent them from tipping, arrange the oysters on a rack or a bed of coarse salt in a shallow pan. Spoon a little of the sauce over each oyster. Broil the oysters 2 inches from the heat for 30 seconds, or until the sauce is lightly browned.

"It is proven by experience that, above five or six dozen, oysters certainly cease to be a pleasure."
Grimod De La Reynière,
Almanach des Gourmands

CHEESY SCALLOPED OYSTERS

Scalloped oysters are a traditional starter for a Thanksgiving or Christmas dinner.

Serves 4

1 cup crushed saltine crackers
½ cup fresh bread crumbs, toasted
¼ cup grated Parmesan cheese
¼ teaspoon dried thyme
4 tablespoons melted unsalted butter
16 shucked oysters (about 1 pint), drained
½ cup heavy cream
½ teaspoon salt
½ teaspoon ground red pepper

1. Preheat the oven to 400° F. Butter a 12 × 8 × 2-inch baking dish or 4 scallop shells.

2. Combine the crackers, bread crumbs, cheese, and thyme and stir in the butter. Spread three-quarters of the crumb mixture in the prepared dish.

3. Arrange the oysters in a single layer over the crumbs. Combine the cream, salt, and pepper and drizzle over the oysters. Top with the remaining crumbs. Bake for 20 minutes, or until the crumbs are golden.

OYSTERS with PARSLEY PESTO

Serves 4

2 dozen oysters on the half shell
½ cup packed fresh parsley leaves
2 tablespoons pine nuts
1 small garlic clove, minced
2 tablespoons grated Parmesan cheese
¼ teaspoon salt
⅛ teaspoon freshly ground black pepper
3 tablespoons olive oil

"Oysters are amatory food."

Lord Byron,
Don Juan

1. Preheat the oven to 350° F. Arrange the oysters on a rack or in a shallow pan filled with coarse salt to prevent them from tipping.

2. In a blender or food processor, combine the parsley, pine nuts, and garlic. Process until finely chopped. Blend in the remaining ingredients.

3. Place a spoonful of parsley mixture on each oyster. Bake for 8 to 10 minutes, until the oysters are plump and heated through.

OYSTERS PICCANTE

Serves 2

1 medium tomato, peeled, seeded, and
    finely chopped
1 scallion, finely chopped
1 small garlic clove, finely chopped
¼ cup chopped fresh coriander
1 to 2 tablespoons finely chopped chilies
¼ teaspoon salt
2 teaspoons olive oil
1 teaspoon white wine vinegar
1 dozen oysters on the half shell
¼ cup fresh bread crumbs

1. In a bowl, combine the tomato, scallion, garlic, coriander, chilies, salt, oil, and vinegar. Let stand at room temperature for 2 hours.

2. Preheat the broiler. To prevent them from tipping, arrange the oysters on a rack or a bed of coarse salt in a shallow pan. Spoon the tomato mixture over the oysters. Sprinkle with the bread crumbs. Broil 4 inches from the heat until the oysters are plump and the crumbs are lightly toasted, about 2 minutes.

Scallops

"Give me my scallop-shell of quiet."

Sir Walter Raleigh

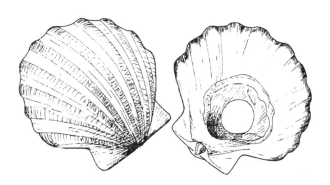

When I was a little girl I used to love to eat at our local fish restaurant. I would always order the same thing—sea scallops crisply fried in a golden crust and served with tangy tartar sauce. Sweet, plump scallops were my favorite shellfish.

Scallops are probably the most beautiful of all shellfish. They have pale pink, fan-shaped shells with scalloped edges. The shells are marked with concentric rings, which are not only decorative but can be used to determine a scallop's age.

Unfortunately, scallop shells do not close tightly, as do oysters, mussels, and hard shell clams, so scallop meat is perishable and can dry out quickly. To preserve them, the scallops are shucked right after they are gathered, and only the large white muscle that opens and closes the shells is removed. This is not the case in Europe and other parts of the world, where the entire contents of the scallop shell are eaten, including the bright coral-colored roe.

Although there are hundreds of varieties of scallops, the most commonly available ones are sea scallops, bay scallops, and calicos. Sea scallops have a fuller flavor and are large, about 1 to 2 inches in diameter. Bay scallops are smaller, about ½ to ¾ inch in diameter, and have a delicate sweet taste. Calicos are similar in size but are often dry, tough, and lacking in flavor. Learn to recognize the difference between bay and calico scallops, since they are sometimes mislabeled in the market, with inexpensive calicos substituted for the more expensive bays. The calicos appear whiter, with a dry outer edge, measuring ¼ to ½ inch in diameter.

One pound of scallops makes 3 to 4 servings. At home, store them in a sealed plastic bag in the refrigerator. Cook them as soon as possible. Depending on their freshness, they should keep for 1 to 2 days. Before cooking, rinse the scallops under cold water and drain well. Pat dry with paper towels.

Thaw frozen scallops in the refrigerator overnight. Sometimes scallops that have been frozen will exude a lot of liquid when they are cooked. This can ruin the delicate crust on fried scallops, so to prevent this, drop the scallops into boiling water for 1 minute. Drain them and pat dry with paper towels. Then proceed with the recipe. Scallops may be fried, baked, broiled, or steamed, but be careful not to overcook them or they will be tough.

BACON GRILLED SCALLOPS

Serves 4

¼ cup bourbon
¼ cup chopped scallions
2 tablespoons maple syrup
1 tablespoon soy sauce
2 teaspoons Dijon mustard
¼ teaspoon freshly ground black pepper
1 pound sea scallops
¼ pound sliced bacon, cut into 3-inch
    lengths

1. In a bowl, combine the bourbon, scallions, maple syrup, soy sauce, mustard, and pepper. Stir in the scallops. Cover and refrigerate for 1 hour.

2. Prepare the grill or heat the broiler. Wrap the scallops in bacon and thread on skewers. Grill or broil 4 inches from the heat, turning once, until the bacon is crisp and the scallops are opaque, about 5 minutes.

SCALLOPS AL PESTO

Serves 6–8

Sauce
1 cup fresh basil leaves
1 large garlic clove
¼ cup pine nuts
½ teaspoon salt
¼ teaspoon freshly ground black pepper
3 tablespoons olive oil

2 pounds sea scallops
3 tablespoons freshly grated Parmesan
    cheese
1 tablespoon fresh bread crumbs

1. In a food processor, finely chop the basil and garlic. Add the nuts and chop finely. Blend in the salt, pepper, and oil.

2. Preheat the oven to 450° F. Lightly oil a 12 × 8 × 2-inch baking dish. Combine the scallops and pesto and spoon into the dish.

3. Combine the cheese and bread crumbs. Sprinkle over the scallops. Bake for 10 minutes, or until the scallops are opaque and the crumbs are lightly browned.

PASTA with SCALLOPS AND PEPPERS

This recipe was inspired by one from a favorite cookbook, *More Classic Italian Cooking* by Marcella Hazan. She bakes the scallop mixture in a gratin dish, but I like it even better served over pasta.

Serves 6

2 large red bell peppers
⅓ cup olive oil
2 large garlic cloves, finely chopped
1 pound bay or sea scallops, cut into
     ½-inch pieces
1 teaspoon salt
¼ teaspoon freshly ground black pepper
¼ cup finely chopped fresh parsley
3 tablespoons drained capers, finely
     chopped
1 pound linguine

1. Roast the peppers by broiling them or turning them frequently over a gas flame until the skin is charred and blistered. Let them cool, then strip off the skin. Remove the cores and seeds. Cut the peppers into narrow 1-inch strips.

2. In a large skillet, heat the oil over medium heat. Stir in the garlic and sauté for 30 seconds. Add the scallops, salt, and pepper. Cook, stirring frequently, until the scallops are no longer translucent, about 3 minutes. Stir in the parsley, capers, and peppers. Cook for 1 minute more.

3. In a large pot of boiling salted water, cook the linguine until firm yet tender to the bite. Drain well and toss with the scallop mixture.

"How many times have I nearly wept at the destruction of delicate little scallops at the hands of ignorant or insensitive chefs."

Elizabeth David,
An Omelette and a Glass of Wine

SZECHUAN SCALLOPS

Serves 4

2 tablespoons peanut or corn oil
1 tablespoon minced garlic
1 tablespoon minced fresh gingerroot
1 pound sea scallops, halved or
    quartered if large
2 tablespoons soy sauce
3 scallions, cut into ½-inch diagonal
    slices
1 to 2 teaspoons Oriental chili paste
2 teaspoons cornstarch dissolved in 3
    tablespoons cold water

1. In a large skillet or wok, heat the oil over high heat. Add the garlic and ginger and cook, stirring constantly, for 30 seconds.

2. Add the scallops, soy sauce, and scallions and cook, stirring, for 2 to 3 minutes, or until the scallops become opaque.

3. Stir in the chili paste. Blend together the cornstarch and water and stir into the scallops. Cook, stirring, until thickened, about 1 minute.

SAUTEED SCALLOPS

To ensure a crisp coating on the scallops, roll them in bread crumbs at the very last moment before sautéing.

Serves 4

⅔ cup fine dry bread crumbs
½ teaspoon paprika
½ teaspoon salt
¼ teaspoon freshly ground black pepper
1 pound sea scallops
4 tablespoons butter
2 tablespoons vegetable oil
Lemon wedges
Tartar Sauce (page 93)

1. On a piece of waxed paper, combine the bread crumbs, paprika, salt, and pepper. Roll the scallops in the bread crumb mixture.

2. In a large skillet, melt the butter with the oil over medium heat. Add the scallops and cook until golden brown, about 2 minutes on each side. Serve with lemon wedges and tartar sauce.

SCALLOPS IN MUSHROOM SAUCE

Serves 4

3 tablespoons butter
2 tablespoons corn oil
1 pound bay or sea scallops, quartered if
    large
Salt
Freshly ground white pepper
2 tablespoons finely chopped shallots or
    onions
1 large garlic clove, finely chopped
8 ounces small mushrooms, thinly sliced
½ cup dry white wine
2 medium tomatoes, peeled, seeded, and
    finely chopped
2 tablespoons finely chopped fresh
    parsley

1. In a large skillet, melt 2 tablespoons butter with the oil over medium heat. Add the scallops and cook, stirring frequently, until opaque, about 2 to 3 minutes. With a slotted spoon, transfer the scallops to a dish. Sprinkle with salt and pepper to taste.

2. Add the remaining butter to the skillet. Stir in the shallots and garlic. Cook for 1 minute. Add the mushrooms and cook, stirring frequently, until lightly browned, about 5 minutes.

3. Add the wine, tomatoes, and parsley and bring to a simmer. Cook for 5 minutes, or until most of the liquid has evaporated. Return the scallops to the skillet and stir gently. Cook for 2 to 3 minutes, until heated through. Taste for seasoning.

SCALLOP, GRAPEFRUIT, AND AVOCADO SALAD

Serves 4

Dressing
½ cup freshly squeezed grapefruit juice
3 tablespoons vegetable oil
1 tablespoon snipped fresh chives
1 tablespoon chopped fresh parsley
1 tablespoon chopped fresh mint
2 teaspoons lemon juice
2 teaspoons Dijon mustard
½ teaspoon salt
⅛ teaspoon freshly ground black pepper

1 teaspoon salt
1 pound bay scallops or quartered sea
    scallops
1 small head Boston lettuce
1 cup grapefruit sections
2 small avocados, peeled, pitted, and
    thinly sliced
Whole chives

1. In a small bowl, whisk together the dressing ingredients. Set aside.

2. In a large saucepan, bring 6 cups water to a boil. Add the salt and scallops. Cook over low heat for 2 minutes, or just until the scallops are opaque. Drain well. Place the scallops in a bowl and toss with half of the dressing. Cover and refrigerate for 2 hours.

3. When ready to serve, arrange the lettuce leaves on 4 plates. Spoon the scallop mixture onto the lettuce. Garnish with grapefruit sections, avocado slices, and whole chives. Drizzle with the remaining dressing.

SCALLOPS with LEMON AND WALNUTS

Serves 4

2 tablespoons unsalted butter
2 tablespoons olive oil
1 pound bay or sea scallops, halved or
    quartered if large
2 tablespoons finely chopped shallots or
    scallion
½ cup coarsely chopped toasted walnuts
2 tablespoons finely chopped fresh
    parsley
½ teaspoon grated lemon zest
½ teaspoon salt
¼ teaspoon freshly ground black pepper

1. In a large skillet, melt the butter with the oil over medium heat. Pat the scallops dry with paper towels and add to the skillet. Cook, stirring, for 2 to 3 minutes.

2. Stir in the shallots. Add the walnuts, parsley, lemon zest, salt, and pepper and cook for 1 minute more.

SCALLOP SHELLS

Scallop shells are more than just a covering for the beautiful bivalve. In medieval Spain they were the emblem of pilgrims visiting the shrine of Santiago de Campostela, said to be the burial place of St. James, one of the twelve apostles of Christ. They have been admired by great artists who painted them, as in Botticelli's *Venus*, which depicts the goddess of love standing in a scallop shell. The French use the name coquilles St. Jacques, meaning St. James shells, to describe both scallops and many dishes made from them.

In culinary terminology, the word *scalloped* is applied to recipes that can be cooked in scallop shells (see Cheesy Scalloped Oysters on page 61). Scallop shells make elegant serving containers for a variety of foods that have nothing to do with scallops. Caribbean Deviled Crabs (page 32) and Mediterranean Mussel and Potato Salad (page 48) are just two of the recipes in this book that would be attractive served in scallop shells.

Sets of scallop shells, usually four to a package, can be bought at most kitchenware stores and are very inexpensive. Wash them well in hot soapy water before using. If the food is to be baked in the shell, butter the insides of the shells before filling. To serve, place the shells on serving dishes. The shells are reusable and can even be washed in the dishwasher.

SPICY FRIED SCALLOPS with SHERRY MAYONNAISE

Serves 4

½ cup all-purpose flour
½ teaspoon paprika
¼ teaspoon baking powder
¼ teaspoon salt
¼ teaspoon ground red pepper
¼ teaspoon freshly ground white pepper
¼ teaspoon freshly ground black pepper
1 garlic clove, crushed
½ to ⅔ cup ice water
1 pound bay scallops or quartered sea
    scallops

Sherry Mayonnaise
½ cup mayonnaise
2 teaspoons dry sherry
¼ teaspoon ground red pepper

Oil for deep frying
Lemon wedges

1. In a bowl, combine the flour, paprika, baking powder, salt, peppers, garlic, and enough ice water to make a thick batter. Stir in the scallops. Cover and refrigerate for 2 hours.

2. In a small bowl, combine all the mayonnaise ingredients and refrigerate until ready to use.

3. In a deep fryer or heavy deep saucepan, heat the oil to 375° F. Carefully slip the scallops into the oil, one at a time. Do not crowd the pan. Fry until the scallops are golden brown, about 3 minutes. Remove with a slotted spoon. Drain on paper towels. Repeat with the remaining scallops. Serve with lemon wedges and sherry mayonnaise.

SCALLOPS PROVENÇALE

Serve with toasted French bread rubbed with fresh garlic.

Serves 3–4

¼ cup olive oil
1 cup chopped onion or ½ cup chopped
    leek plus ½ cup chopped onion
4 plum tomatoes or 1 large tomato,
    peeled, seeded, and chopped
2 garlic cloves, finely chopped
½ cup dry white wine
½ cup clam juice
1½-inch strip orange zest
1 bay leaf
1 teaspoon chopped fresh thyme or ¼
    teaspoon dried
½ teaspoon salt
¼ teaspoon freshly ground black pepper
¼ teaspoon fennel seeds
Pinch of saffron
1 pound bay or sea scallops, quartered if
    large
2 tablespoons finely chopped fresh
    parsley

1. In a large skillet, heat the oil over medium heat. Add the onion and sauté until softened, about 5 minutes.

2. Stir in the tomatoes and garlic and cook for 5 minutes more. Add the wine, clam juice, orange zest, bay leaf, thyme, salt, pepper, fennel, and saffron and bring to a simmer. Cook for 30 minutes.

3. Stir in the scallops. Cook for 2 to 3 minutes, or until the scallops are opaque. Spoon into soup bowls and garnish with parsley.

Shrimp

"I shall be but a shrimp of an author."

Thomas Gray

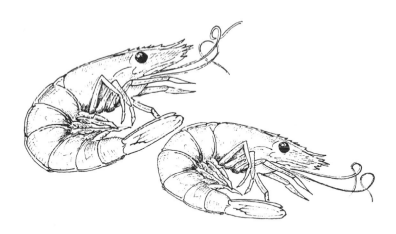

More shrimp are eaten in North America than any other shellfish. Fried, baked, grilled, or broiled, shrimp are probably the most adaptable variety.

The term *green* is sometimes used to describe raw shrimp, but it has nothing to do with appearance. Uncooked shrimp vary in color from grayish white to light brown. They all taste pretty much the same, and all turn pink or red with white flesh when cooked.

Because shrimp deteriorate quickly once they are caught, their heads are removed and the tails are flash frozen. In the market, headless shrimp are sold either frozen or thawed, in the shell or out. Whole fresh shrimp that have never been frozen are sometimes available, but frozen, thawed shrimp can be very good.

When purchasing, look for plump shrimp with shells securely attached. They should be firm and there should be no black spots on the shell. The smell should be fresh, with no trace of ammonia. At home, keep them well chilled. Thaw frozen shrimp overnight in the refrigerator or under cold running water, changing the water often. Use shrimp a day or two after purchasing.

Shrimp are available in a variety of sizes, from "tiny" to "extra-colossal." For most recipes, medium shrimp averaging 30 to the pound are a good size. For stuffed shrimp, butterflied shrimp, or a fancy shrimp cocktail, large or jumbo shrimp would be a better choice.

Purchase 1½ pounds shrimp in the shell for 4 servings.

Some cooks feel that shrimp taste better when they are cooked in the shell. This makes eating the shrimp difficult, however, and the flavor difference is minimal. I usually peel them first, but the choice is up to you.

To peel, hold a shrimp in one hand with the legs up. With the thumb and forefinger of the other hand, peel off the shell two or three sections at a time, beginning at the head end. The last section can be left attached, as a handle, or removed by gently pulling on the tail.

It is not necessary to devein shrimp, but they will look better if you do. With a small sharp knife, make a shallow cut lengthwise down the back of each shrimp. Pull out the vein or rinse the shrimp under cool water to remove.

PERFECT BOILED SHRIMP

Onions, celery, lemon slices, or herbs can be added to the cooking water to further season the shrimp. Serve with Cocktail Sauce (page 92).

Serves 4

1 pound medium shrimp, shelled and deveined
1 teaspoon salt

1. Bring 2 quarts of water to a boil. Add the shrimp and salt. Cook for 2 to 3 minutes, or until the shrimp are opaque.

2. Place the shrimp in a strainer and run under cold water for 1 to 2 minutes, or until cooled. Chill until serving time.

SHRIMP SCAMPI

Serve these shrimp with rice or crispy bread to soak up the delicious sauce.

Serves 4

4 tablespoons unsalted butter
¼ cup olive oil
1 tablespoon finely chopped garlic
½ cup dry white wine
2 tablespoons lemon juice
1 pound medium shrimp, shelled and deveined
2 tablespoons chopped fresh parsley
½ teaspoon salt
¼ teaspoon freshly ground black pepper

1. Preheat the broiler. In a large skillet with a flameproof handle, melt the butter with the oil over medium heat. Add the garlic and sauté for 30 seconds. Stir in the wine and lemon juice and cook for 1 minute. Remove from the heat. Stir in the shrimp, parsley, salt, and pepper. Spread the shrimp in a single layer.

2. Broil the shrimp just until pink, about 3 minutes.

SONOMA SHRIMP

I never used to like dried tomatoes because the quality of the imported ones was so unreliable. Now, however, I can find excellent dried tomatoes from California at my local supermarket. The intense tomato flavor marries well with shellfish, especially shrimp, scallops, and squid.

Serves 3–4

½ cup dried tomatoes
¼ cup olive oil
4 scallions, thinly sliced
1 garlic clove, finely chopped
1 pound medium shrimp, shelled and
　　deveined
1 tablespoon all-purpose flour
½ teaspoon crumbled dried rosemary
¼ cup dry sherry
Salt
Freshly ground black pepper

1. Soak the tomatoes in warm water to cover for 2 minutes. Drain and pat dry. Cut into thin strips.

2. In a large skillet, heat the oil over medium heat. Add the scallions and garlic and sauté until tender, about 3 minutes.

3. Toss the shrimp with the flour. Add the shrimp, tomatoes, and rosemary to the skillet. Cook, turning once, until the shrimp turn pink, about 2 minutes.

4. Stir in the sherry and salt and pepper to taste, and bring to a simmer. Reduce the heat to low. Cook until most of the liquid evaporates and the shrimp are cooked through.

DEVILED SHRIMP

Serves 4

½ cup finely chopped scallions
¼ cup chopped fresh parsley
½ teaspoon dried thyme
¼ teaspoon freshly ground black pepper
⅓ cup Dijon mustard
3 tablespoons dry white wine or
    vermouth
2 tablespoons lemon juice
2 tablespoons olive oil
1½ pounds medium shrimp, shelled and
    deveined
2 tablespoons bread crumbs

1. Preheat the oven to 400° F. Lightly oil a 12 × 9-inch shallow baking pan.

2. In a small bowl, combine the scallions, parsley, thyme, pepper, mustard, wine, lemon juice, and oil. Dip the shrimp in the mixture and place them in a single layer in the baking pan. Sprinkle with the bread crumbs.

3. Bake for 5 minutes, or until the shrimp are pink and the bread crumbs lightly browned.

COCONUT SHRIMP

In Florida, these are served with honey mustard instead of chutney.

Serves 4

2 cups shredded coconut
1 cup fresh bread crumbs
2 eggs
½ cup all-purpose flour
Chutney
1 teaspoon salt
Freshly ground white pepper
1 pound medium shrimp, shelled and
    deveined
Vegetable oil for deep frying

1. On a piece of waxed paper, combine the coconut and bread crumbs.

2. In a shallow dish, beat the eggs with the flour, 2 tablespoons chopped chutney, salt, and pepper to taste. Dip the shrimp in the egg mixture and roll them in the coconut mixture. Place the shrimp on a rack and let dry for 15 minutes.

3. In a deep fryer or heavy deep saucepan, heat the oil to 375°F. Cook the shrimp, turning once, until crisp and browned, about 4 minutes. Drain on paper towels. Keep cooked shrimp warm in a low oven while frying the remaining shrimp. Serve with additional chutney.

SHRIMP, CORN, AND CHILI SALAD

Serves 4

3 medium ears of corn or 1 package (10 ounces) frozen corn kernels
1 pound medium shrimp, shelled and deveined
3 tablespoons corn oil
3 tablespoons lemon juice
1 teaspoon salt
¼ teaspoon freshly ground black pepper
½ teaspoon oregano
½ teaspoon ground cumin
1 pint cherry tomatoes, halved
6 scallions, finely chopped
½ cup chopped fresh coriander
2 to 3 tablespoons finely chopped jalapeño pepper
Romaine lettuce leaves

1. Remove the husks and silk from the corn and, with a knife, scrape the kernels from the cobs into a bowl. In a small saucepan, bring 2 cups of water to a boil. Add the corn kernels, cover, and cook for 4 minutes, or until tender. If using frozen corn kernels, cook according to package directions. Drain well and allow to cool slightly.

2. In a large saucepan, bring 6 cups of water to a boil. Add the shrimp and cook just until opaque in the center, about 2 minutes. Drain well.

3. In a large bowl, combine the oil, lemon juice, salt, black pepper, oregano, and cumin. Add the shrimp and toss to coat.

4. Stir in the corn, tomatoes, scallions, coriander, and jalapeño. Serve on lettuce leaves.

ITALIAN GRILLED SHRIMP

Serves 4

¼ cup olive oil
¼ cup lemon juice
¼ cup chopped fresh parsley
2 large garlic cloves, minced
½ teaspoon dried oregano
½ teaspoon grated lemon zest
½ teaspoon salt
⅛ teaspoon freshly ground black pepper
1 pound medium shrimp, shelled and
    deveined
¼ cup fine dry bread crumbs

1. In a medium bowl, combine the oil, lemon juice, parsley, garlic, oregano, lemon zest, salt, and pepper. Add the shrimp and toss well. Cover and refrigerate for 1 hour.

2. Prepare the grill or preheat the broiler. Thread the shrimp on four 12-inch metal or bamboo skewers. Sprinkle with bread crumbs. Grill or broil, turning once, for 4 to 6 minutes, or until the shrimp are opaque in the center.

MARINATED SHRIMP

Serves 4

1 celery stalk, coarsely chopped
1 carrot, peeled and coarsely chopped
1 small onion, quartered
1 teaspoon salt
1 bay leaf
1½ pounds small to medium shrimp,
    peeled and deveined
½ cup olive oil
¼ cup lemon juice
1 large garlic clove, finely chopped
½ teaspoon oregano
¼ teaspoon freshly ground black pepper

1. In a medium saucepan, bring 2 quarts of water to a boil. Add the celery, carrot, onion, salt, and bay leaf. Simmer for 10 minutes.

2. Add the shrimp. Cook for 1 to 2 minutes after the water returns to a simmer, or until the shrimp are opaque in the center. Drain.

3. In a medium bowl, combine the oil, lemon juice, garlic, oregano, and pepper. Stir in the shrimp. Cover and marinate for at least 1 hour. Serve at room temperature.

GINGER GRILLED SHRIMP

These make wonderful party appetizers served on short bamboo skewers.

Serves 3–4

¼ cup soy sauce
¼ cup chopped scallions
2 tablespoons sesame oil
2 garlic cloves, finely chopped
1 tablespoon minced fresh gingerroot
Pinch of ground red pepper
1 pound medium shrimp, shelled and
    deveined

1. In a medium bowl, combine the soy sauce, scallions, oil, garlic, ginger, and pepper. Stir in the shrimp and coat well. Cover and refrigerate for several hours or overnight.

2. Preheat the broiler or prepare the grill. Thread the shrimp on skewers. Broil or grill just until shrimp turn pink and are opaque in the center.

SHRIMP IN GREEN SAUCE

Serves 4

¼ cup olive oil
1½ pounds medium shrimp, shelled and
    deveined
Salt
Freshly ground black pepper
4 garlic cloves, finely chopped
⅓ cup finely chopped scallions
1½ tablespoons all-purpose flour
1 bottle (8 ounces) clam juice
½ cup dry white wine
½ cup finely chopped fresh parsley
1 cup cooked peas
½ teaspoon crushed red pepper

1. In a large skillet, heat the oil over medium heat. Add the shrimp and sauté just until pink, about 2 minutes. With a slotted spoon, transfer the shrimp to a bowl. Season to taste with salt and black pepper.

2. Add the garlic and scallions to the skillet and cook, stirring, for 2 minutes. Stir in the flour and cook for 1 minute more. Gradually blend in the clam juice and wine. Bring to a simmer and cook until slightly thickened, about 2 minutes. Stir in the parsley, peas, red pepper, and salt and pepper to taste. Return the shrimp to the skillet and cook, stirring, until heated through, about 2 minutes.

SHRIMP CURRY

For a more elaborate presentation, pass the curry with garnishes of chopped peanuts, chutney, and sliced scallions.

Serves 4

4 tablespoons unsalted butter
1½ pounds medium shrimp, shelled and deveined
½ cup chopped peeled apple
½ cup chopped onion
1 garlic clove, finely chopped
2 tablespoons all-purpose flour
1 tablespoon curry powder
¼ teaspoon freshly ground white pepper
⅛ teaspoon ground nutmeg
1 cup clam juice or chicken broth
½ cup heavy cream
Hot cooked rice

1. In a large skillet, melt 2 tablespoons butter over medium heat. Add the shrimp and cook, stirring constantly, until they turn pink, about 2 minutes. Remove the shrimp to a bowl.

2. In same skillet, melt the remaining butter over medium-low heat. Add the apple, onion, and garlic. Cook just until tender, about 5 minutes. Stir in the flour, curry powder, pepper, and nutmeg. Cook for 4 minutes more.

3. Slowly stir in the clam juice and cream. Bring to a simmer. Add the shrimp and cook for 1 to 2 minutes, or until heated. Serve with hot cooked rice.

"Listen, Joe, as long as you're here, why don't you just sit yourself down on the floor over there and peel this pile of shrimp?"

Calvin Trillin,
Third Helpings

SHRIMP IN BEER

These shrimp are perfect for a backyard party. Since guests shell their own, make sure you have plenty of napkins on hand and provide a bowl for the shells. The shrimp also taste great cold, served with mayonnaise or tartar sauce.

Serves 3–4

Sauce
½ cup (1 stick) melted unsalted butter
1 teaspoon lemon juice
4 or 5 drops hot red pepper sauce

1 pound medium shrimp
2 bottles (12 ounces each) beer
1 large onion, thinly sliced
1 teaspoon salt
1 teaspoon celery seed
1 bay leaf
½ teaspoon dried thyme
3 or 4 drops hot red pepper sauce

1. In a small saucepan, melt the butter over low heat. Add the lemon juice and hot pepper sauce. Keep warm while preparing the shrimp.

2. Wash the shrimp but leave the shells on. In a large saucepan, combine the beer, onion, salt, celery seed, bay leaf, thyme, and hot pepper sauce. Bring to a boil and cook for 5 minutes.

3. Add the shrimp and return to a boil. Reduce the heat and simmer for 2 to 5 minutes, or until the shrimp are opaque in the center. Drain the shrimp and serve hot with the butter sauce.

Squid

"Ah, but who can tell the mind of a squid?"
John Gillespie

Squid, also known as calamari, are one of the least appreciated of all varieties of shellfish. This may be changing as shellfish lovers learn that squid are truly delicious and adaptable to all kinds of cooking. What's more, they cost a fraction of most other seafood.

The squid is a strange-looking creature with a long tubular body and a head topped with ten tentacles. Purplish pink mottled skin covers the entire animal. Unlike other shellfish, the shell of the squid is located *inside* the body, in the form of a clear, plastic-looking piece called a pen. Because they have the ability to move rapidly both backward and forward, squid have gained a reputation for erratic behavior. They are equipped with ink sacs, which they empty in the face of pursuing enemies, like one of James Bond's smokescreens. Some Spanish and Italian recipes call for cooking squid in their ink, which makes a savory sauce. These may be difficult to replicate on this side of the Atlantic, however, because the ink sac is usually removed before the squid reach the fish market.

Large squid are good for stuffing, while smaller varieties can be boiled, stewed, or fried. Squid are available fresh and frozen, cleaned and uncleaned. When buying cleaned squid, make sure that they have a pearly, moist surface and show no signs of yellowing. Their aroma should be fresh and mild. It is rare to find a fish market that does a really thorough job of cleaning squid, so be prepared to look them over and finish the cleaning at home.

Thaw frozen squid in a bowl of cold water, changing the water frequently. Use as soon as possible after thawing or purchasing, preferably the same day. Buy about ⅔ pound of uncleaned or ½ pound cleaned squid per serving.

Cooked in boiling water for 45 seconds, then drained and rinsed in cold water to stop the cooking, squid are tender and perfect for salads. For stewed or baked recipes, squid are cooked for at least 20 minutes, at which time they become tender, but will shrink in size. Pan- or deep-fried squid need about 2 minutes to brown. So the rule of thumb is to cook squid either very quickly or rather slowly—under 1 minute for boiled, 2 minutes for fried, over 20 minutes for stewed or stuffed, etc. Anywhere in between, they are as tough and chewy as rubber bands.

To clean squid, hold the body of the squid in one hand and the head and tentacles in the other. Gently pull the two apart. Cut off the tentacles just above the eyes. Discard the lower portion. Squeeze the base of the tentacles to extract the hard beak. Set the tentacles aside. Pull out the pen or quill, a long, clear shell inside the body. Hold the body like a tube of toothpaste and squeeze out and discard the jellylike viscera. Removing the skin is optional. To do so, pull off as much as possible with your fingers. Use a small knife to scrape off the rest. Rinse squid thoroughly, inside and out. Drain well and pat dry.

STUFFED CALAMARI

Serves 6–8

16 large squid (about 2½ pounds),
    cleaned
9 tablespoons olive oil
1 medium onion, chopped
2 small zucchini, chopped
1 large red bell pepper, seeded and
    chopped
1 teaspoon salt
¼ teaspoon freshly ground black pepper
¼ cup toasted bread crumbs
Pinch of rosemary
1 cup dry white wine

1. Set the squid bodies aside. Finely chop the tentacles (a food processor does this easily).

2. In a large skillet, heat 3 tablespoons oil. Add the onion and sauté until tender, about 10 minutes. Add the chopped tentacles, zucchini, red pepper, salt, and black pepper. Cook for 10 minutes, or until most of the juices evaporate. Remove from the heat and stir in the bread crumbs. Let cool.

3. Loosely stuff the bodies with some of the vegetable mixture. Do not add too much stuffing, or it will ooze out during cooking. With toothpicks, close up the squid at each end.

4. Put 3 tablespoons oil in each of two large skillets. Heat over medium heat. Add the squid and rosemary and cook until the squid are lightly browned, turning occasionally. Divide the wine between the skillets and bring to a boil. Cook for 1 minute. Reduce the heat to a simmer, cover the skillets, and cook for 1 hour, or until the squid are tender.

5. Remove the picks. Place the squid on a warm serving platter, pour the cooking liquid over, and serve immediately.

MEXICAN SQUID SALAD

This light, refreshing salad is very low in calories.

Serves 4–6

2 pounds cleaned squid
2 teaspoons salt
3 tablespoons olive oil
¼ cup fresh lime juice
2 tablespoons chopped fresh coriander
¼ teaspoon ground cumin
¼ teaspoon freshly ground black pepper
6 cups torn salad greens
1 medium tomato, diced
1 small ripe avocado, peeled and diced

1. Cut the squid bodies into ½-inch rings. Cut the tentacles in half.

2. Bring 3 quarts of water to a boil. Add 1 teaspoon salt and the squid. Boil for 45 seconds, just until the squid turn opaque. Drain and run under cold water to stop the cooking. Drain well.

3. In a bowl, combine the oil, lime juice, coriander, cumin, pepper, and 1 teaspoon salt. Add the squid and stir to coat. Cover and chill for up to 3 hours.

4. Arrange the salad greens on 4 serving plates. Toss the squid with the tomato and avocado. Spoon over the greens and serve immediately.

STIR-FRIED SQUID

Serves 2

1 pound cleaned squid
¼ cup peanut or corn oil
4 scallions, trimmed and cut into ½-inch lengths
1 tablespoon finely chopped fresh gingerroot
1 garlic clove, finely chopped
2 tablespoons soy sauce
2 tablespoons dry sherry
1 teaspoon cornstarch
1 tablespoon water

1. Cut the squid into ½-inch-wide rings. Cut the tentacles in half.

2. In a large wok or skillet, heat the oil over medium-high heat. Add the squid, scallions, ginger, and garlic. Cook, stirring, for 1 minute. Add the soy sauce and sherry and cook, stirring for 2 minutes more.

3. In a small dish, dissolve the cornstarch in the water. Stir the cornstarch into the squid mixture and cook until the sauce thickens and clears, about 1 minute more. Serve with rice.

SAUTEED SQUID with PEPPERS

This makes a good, if unusual, sandwich filling on crusty Italian bread. Serve it hot or at room temperature.

Serves 2

¼ cup olive oil
1 large onion, chopped
1 large red pepper, seeded and thinly sliced
1 large green pepper, seeded and thinly sliced
1 teaspoon salt
½ teaspoon oregano
¼ teaspoon ground red pepper
1 pound cleaned squid, cut into 1-inch pieces

1. In a large skillet, heat the oil over medium heat. Add the onion and peppers and cook, stirring occasionally, until tender and lightly browned, about 20 minutes. Stir in the salt, oregano, and ground pepper.

2. Raise the heat to medium-high. Stir in the squid and cook just until the squid becomes opaque, about 2 minutes.

"Do you speak squidish?"

Kermit the Frog

SQUID IN WHITE WINE

Serves 4

¼ cup olive oil
2 garlic cloves, minced
½ cup finely chopped scallions
2 pounds cleaned squid, cut into ½-inch-wide rings
1 cup dry white wine
1 teaspoon salt
Freshly ground black pepper
2 cups fresh or thawed frozen peas

1. In a large skillet, heat the oil over medium heat. Add the garlic and scallions and cook, stirring, for 2 minutes.

2. Stir in the squid and wine. Cover and simmer for 20 minutes. Add the salt, pepper to taste, and peas. Simmer uncovered for 5 minutes more, or until most of the liquid evaporates.

CALAMARI DORE

This recipe was given to me by Horace Mercurio, owner of Moss Landing Oyster Bar in Moss Landing, California, not far from Salinas. It is an informal place, always packed, that serves fabulous fresh fish and shellfish.

Pounding the squid is necessary both to tenderize it and to prevent it from curling up as it cooks. But even if it does curl, it still tastes delicious. If only small squid are available, double or triple the amount.

Serves 6

1 cup all-purpose flour
¼ teaspoon salt
¼ teaspoon freshly ground black pepper
3 eggs
6 large cleaned squid (5 to 6 ounces each)
¼ cup olive oil
4 tablespoons unsalted butter
½ small garlic clove, minced
3 tablespoons lemon juice
2 tablespoons chopped fresh parsley

1. On a sheet of waxed paper, combine the flour, salt, and pepper. In a shallow bowl, beat the eggs until frothy.

2. Set aside the squid tentacles for another use. Slit the bodies lengthwise and open flat. Place the squid between two sheets of plastic wrap. With a meat mallet or the bottom of a small saucepan, gently pound the squid all over to flatten them slightly. With a small knife, make several ½-inch slits around the edges.

3. Coat the squid lightly on both sides with the flour, then dip into the eggs.

4. In a large heavy skillet, heat the oil over medium-high heat. The oil should be very hot. Test it by dropping a bit of the egg mixture into the pan. It should sizzle and puff immediately. Lay a squid flat in the skillet. Place a metal spatula or a flat saucepan lid on top to prevent curling. Cook until golden brown, about 2 minutes on each side. Place on a heated serving platter and keep warm while cooking the rest of the squid.

5. When all the squid are cooked, wipe out the skillet with a paper towel. Add the butter, garlic, lemon juice, and parsley. Cook, swirling, just until the butter is melted. Pour the sauce over the squid and serve immediately.

CALAMARI with MUSHROOMS

Serves 4

⅓ cup olive oil
1 medium onion, finely chopped
1 garlic clove, finely chopped
8 ounces mushrooms, quartered if large
2 pounds cleaned squid, cut into
    ½-inch-wide rings
1 can (28 ounces) Italian peeled tomatoes
    with their juice, finely chopped
¼ cup finely chopped fresh parsley
1 teaspoon crumbled dried rosemary
1 teaspoon salt
Freshly ground black pepper

1. In a large skillet, heat the oil over medium heat. Add the onion and cook until tender, about 5 minutes. Stir in the garlic.

2. Add the mushrooms. Cook, stirring frequently, until most of the liquid evaporates, about 10 minutes.

3. Stir in the squid, tomatoes, parsley, rosemary, salt, and pepper. Reduce the heat to low. Cover and simmer for 20 minutes, or until the squid is tender and the sauce thickened.

FRIED SQUID

Squid can be fried in batter, like the scallops on page 71, or dipped in beaten eggs and bread crumbs, but they are at their light and crispy best when fried in a dusting of flour. Be sure to flour them at the last moment, or they may become gummy.

Serves 4

Oil for deep frying
2 pounds cleaned squid, cut into
    ¼-inch-wide rings
1 cup all-purpose flour

Salt
Lemon wedges

1. In a deep fryer or heavy deep saucepan, heat the oil to 375° F.

2. Dry the squid with paper towels. Dip the squid, a few pieces at a time, in the flour and shake to remove the excess. Working with small batches, gently lower the squid into the hot oil. Do not fry too many pieces at one time, or they may stick together. Remove the squid with a slotted spoon and drain on paper towels. Place on a hot platter and keep warm while frying the rest. Sprinkle with salt and serve with lemon wedges.

SQUID with CELERY AND OLIVES

Use the tender celery stalks found in the center of the head for this refreshing salad. I love the contrast of the crunchy celery with the chewy squid. Other shellfish, such as shrimp or mussels, can be added to this salad.

Serves 4

2 pounds cleaned squid
1/3 cup olive oil
3 tablespoons red wine vinegar
1 garlic clove, finely chopped
1/2 teaspoon oregano
1/2 teaspoon salt
1/4 teaspoon freshly ground black pepper
2 stalks celery, thinly sliced
1/2 cup sliced green olives
2 tablespoons chopped fresh parsley
Radicchio or red leaf lettuce

1. Cut the squid into 1/2-inch-wide rings. Cut the tentacles in half. Bring a large saucepan of water to a boil. Add the squid and cook just until opaque, about 45 seconds. Drain and rinse under cold water. Drain again.

2. In a large bowl, whisk together the oil, vinegar, garlic, oregano, salt, and pepper. Stir in the squid, celery, olives, and parsley. Cover and chill for at least 1 hour before serving on a bed of radicchio or lettuce leaves.

"We ate one, called a calamaro in Italy, and discovered that it has a remarkable resemblance to fried calf's ear."

Alexandre Dumas

SPAGHETTI with SPICY SQUID SAUCE

Make this sauce as hot or as mild as you like by adjusting the amount of red pepper.

Serves 6–8

⅓ cup olive oil
2 large garlic cloves, finely chopped
½ teaspoon crushed red pepper
2 pounds cleaned squid, cut into 1-inch
    pieces
½ cup dry white wine
1 can (28 ounces) Italian peeled
    tomatoes, chopped and juices
    reserved
1 teaspoon salt
¼ teaspoon freshly ground black pepper
1 pound spaghetti

1. In a large pot, heat the oil over medium heat. Stir in the garlic and red pepper.

2. Add the squid and sauté for 3 minutes. Raise the heat to high and stir in the wine. Cook for 1 minute.

3. Reduce the heat to low. Add the tomatoes with their juice, the salt, and the pepper. Bring to a simmer and cook for 1 hour, or until the squid is tender and the sauce is thick.

4. Cook the spaghetti in a large pot of boiling salted water until tender yet firm to the bite. Drain well and toss with the squid and sauce.

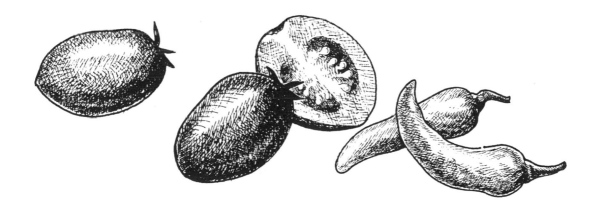

Sauces

DILL CREAM

Serve with cold shrimp, scallops, or lobster.

Makes ⅔ cup

½ cup sour cream
1 tablespoon heavy cream
1 tablespoon fresh dill or 1 teaspoon dried
1 tablespoon lemon juice
¼ teaspoon salt
Freshly ground white pepper to taste

In a blender or food processor, combine all ingredients and process until smooth. Chill until ready to serve.

COCKTAIL SAUCE

Grated onion and Worcestershire sauce are sometimes added for more zest. Use this with clams or mussels on the half shell or boiled shrimp.

Makes 1 cup

½ cup chili sauce
½ cup ketchup
1 tablespoon lemon juice
1 to 2 tablespoons prepared horseradish
2 or 3 drops hot red pepper sauce

Combine all the ingredients. Chill until ready to serve.

CHINESE HOT SAUCE

Serve this sauce with steamed clams or mussels.

Makes ¾ cup

2 tablespoons peanut or corn oil
½ cup soy sauce
2 tablespoons chopped fresh chili pepper
1 tablespoon sesame oil
1 tablespoon white vinegar

Combine all the ingredients. Let stand at room temperature for 1 hour before serving.

TARTAR SAUCE

Serve with fried scallops, shrimp, or squid.

Makes 1¼ cups

1 cup mayonnaise
2 tablespoons finely chopped sour pickles
1 tablespoon finely chopped capers
1 tablespoon grated onion
1 tablespoon finely chopped fresh
    parsley or tarragon
1 to 2 teaspoons lemon juice
1 teaspoon Dijon mustard

Combine all the ingredients. Chill until ready to serve.

REMOULADE SAUCE

Serve with cold or fried shellfish.

Makes 1¼ cups

1 cup mayonnaise
2 tablespoons chopped capers
2 tablespoons chopped sour pickle
2 tablespoons chopped fresh parsley
1 teaspoon Dijon mustard
½ teaspoon anchovy paste or 1 canned
    anchovy, finely chopped

Combine all the ingredients and refrigerate until ready to serve.

FRESH TOMATO SALSA

Good with clams, mussels, or oysters on the half shell.

Makes 2 cups

2 ripe medium tomatoes, seeded and
    chopped
2 to 3 tablespoons minced jalapeño
    peppers
2 tablespoons chopped fresh coriander
2 tablespoons olive oil
1 tablespoon fresh lime juice
½ teaspoon salt

Combine all the ingredients. Let stand at room temperature for 1 hour before serving.

Index